AF630968

Addressing Modern Slavery

Justine Nolan is Associate Professor and Associate Dean in the Faculty of Law at the University of New South Wales. She specialises in business and human rights and supply chain regulation.

Martijn Boersma is Lecturer in the Faculty of Business at the University of Technology Sydney. He is interested in the intersection of business and society and has published widely on these topics.

'Justine Nolan and Martijn Boersma have expertly confronted the tragic reality of modern slavery and show us how exploited men, women and children are harmed in global supply chains. A slave may be far away or in our immediate neighbourhood. The book is based on years of careful research and outlines steps we can all take to respond to modern slavery.' – Jennifer Burn, Professor, NSW Interim Anti-Slavery Commissioner

'This is a hugely impressive book which builds a compelling argument as to why all organisations must work towards the elimination of modern slavery' – David Cooke, Managing Director, Konica Minolta

'The book should be a valuable resource for policymakers, business executives and civil society organisations alike, for it not only assesses the efficacy of existing regulatory initiatives and business practices, but also outlines what needs to change to eliminate modern slavery.' – Surya Deva, City University of Hong Kong

'*Addressing Modern Slavery* is essential reading for anyone committed to understanding and tackling the scourge of modern slavery in contemporary businesses and supply chains.' – Fiona McGaughey, University of Western Australia

'This book exposes both the need and the opportunities to drive reform on modern slavery, particularly on forced labor. From case studies around business practices to examples grounded in the lived experiences of workers, *Addressing Modern Slavery* presents a comprehensive overview of the issue and empowers us all with the information we need to act.' – Amol Mehra, Managing Director, Freedom Fund

'*Addressing Modern Slavery* shines a light on the terrible human cost of our insatiable consumption. Pervasive labour exploitation is all too often forgotten in our emphasis on growth and GDP. This book is both a wake-up call and a powerful demonstration of how connectivity and collaboration can help us eradicate a systemic and urgent challenge.' – Kumi Naidoo, Secretary General, Amnesty International

Justine Nolan and
Martijn Boersma

Addressing Modern Slavery

UNSW PRESS

A UNSW Press book

Published by
NewSouth Publishing
University of New South Wales Press Ltd
University of New South Wales
Sydney NSW 2052
AUSTRALIA
newsouthpublishing.com

© Justine Nolan and Martijn Boersma 2019
First published 2019

10 9 8 7 6 5 4 3 2 1

This book is copyright. Apart from any fair dealing for the purpose of private study, research, criticism or review, as permitted under the Copyright Act, no part of this book may be reproduced by any process without written permission. Inquiries should be addressed to the publisher.

NATIONAL LIBRARY OF AUSTRALIA

A catalogue record for this book is available from the National Library of Australia

ISBN 9781742236438 (paperback)
9781742244631 (ebook)
9781742249124 (epdf)

Design Josephine Pajor-Markus
Cover design Luke Causby, Blue Cork
Cover image aldomurillo/Getty Images
Printer Griffin Press

All reasonable efforts were taken to obtain permission to use copyright material reproduced in this book, but in some cases copyright could not be traced. The authors welcome information in this regard.

This book is printed on paper using fibre supplied from plantation or sustainably managed forests.

UNSW SYDNEY

Contents

1

Modern slavery: A global problem

It is a global goal to eradicate forced labour, end modern slavery and human trafficking, and eliminate the worst forms of child labour by 2030.[1] There are currently an estimated 40.3 million people enslaved around the world, which means around 10 000 people need to escape from slavery each day to achieve this goal.[2] This is a daunting challenge. In recent years, public interest in modern slavery has risen dramatically. Prominent figures such as United Nations Secretary General António Guterres and Pope Francis have committed to fight this 'vile crime'[3] that creates 'a grievous wound in the body of humanity'.[4]

Several countries around the world are increasing their efforts to address modern slavery. The United

Kingdom has observed an Anti-Slavery Day every year since 2010 and introduced its *Modern Slavery Act* in 2015. A similar Act was introduced in Australia in 2018. Modern slavery cases frequently appear in the news, most notably when details are particularly shocking, such as when victims have been 'branded like cattle'.[5] The attention given to modern slavery becomes apparent when examining the increased use of the term in English-language newspapers across the globe, journals and magazines, and on radio and television: modern slavery was mentioned 41 times in 2000, 117 times in 2005, 420 times in 2010, 2130 times in 2015, and 6297 times in 2018.[6]

Despite increasing awareness of modern slavery, some practices remain unchanged. Personal stories of former slaves hundreds of years ago describe the deceptive plots and the use of coercion that underpin the systematic exploitation of human beings. Disturbingly, many of these practices have remained the same over time. While the firsthand accounts of slavery centuries ago supported the push for abolition, modern-day accounts bring to light the harsh reality that enslavement continues to this day.

During the 300 years of transatlantic slave trade, about 12.5 million people were enslaved in the Americas.[7] Today, an estimated 40.3 million people are enslaved globally. That means that there are 5.4 victims of modern slavery for every 1000 people in the world. About 30.4 million in the Asia-Pacific region, 9.1 million people in Africa, and 1.5 million people in developed economies are trapped in modern slavery. Of those enslaved, 16 million are exploited in the private economy, 4.8 million people are in forced sexual exploitation, and 4 million people are exploited by governments.[8] It is estimated that there are at least 136 000 slaves in the UK and 15 000 in Australia.[9] Evidently slavery has not merely endured – it has thrived.

These statistics are not without methodological challenges. As shown in this chapter, there is no universally agreed upon definition of modern slavery. That means that it is not always clear what types of labour abuses should be 'counted' as modern slavery. In addition, there are regional gaps in the data that is available, as there is no globally consistent effort to gather data on modern slavery.

While it is difficult to extrapolate local figures to regional data and global estimates, the frequency with which modern slavery cases are exposed leaves no doubt that addressing forced labour is one of the big challenges of our time.

Our discussion explores why modern slavery continues to this day and focuses on the preponderance of forced labour in activities connected to the mainstream economy. In our contemporary economy, global supply chains separate consumption from production. It has become easy to dismiss modern slavery as something that is not our problem. Yet while lengthy supply chains often originate in remote workplaces – factories, fields

DESPAIR AND DECEPTION

[A merchant] took great notice of my unhappy situation and enquired into the cause; he expressed vast concern for me, and said, if my parents would part with me for a little while, and let him take me home with him, it would be of more service to me than anything they could do for me. I was heartily rejoiced when we arrived at the end of our journey: I now vainly imagined that all my troubles and inquietudes would terminate here; but could I have looked into futurity, I should have perceived that I had much more to suffer than I had before experienced, and that they had as yet but barely commenced.

Ukawsaw Gronniosaw (1772).[10]

I was told I could earn S$1000 a month as a construction worker, but I had to pay S$9000 to the training centre and another S$9000 in agent fees before I could arrive. My family had to sell land, borrow money and even take out a bank loan to pay for it all. I was paid the promised S$1000 a month for the first five months but didn't get any payment for overtime. Then for three months we got no salary at all. We thought our boss would pay us eventually, but then we discovered he'd fled Singapore. We weren't able to make the monthly repayments, so now we're in trouble. There's a 20% fine on the loan, and men from the bank go to my parents' house every day, shouting at them to pay it back. If we still can't pay back the bank, they're going to seize the deeds for my family's land.

Ali, Bangladesh (2018).[11]

or mines – where labour abuses are endemic, modern slavery also occurs close to home.

Modern slavery is a multi-dimensional issue that is often dismissed, underestimated or misunderstood. While modern slavery has only recently become prominent in public debate, exploitative labour practices have developed persistently over time and continue to do so by cleverly adapting to social and economic changes. The fact remains that stories about modern slavery pose uncomfortable truths for businesses and individuals. Regular revelations about modern slavery show that this practice can reach into every aspect of a company's operations and supply chains, as well as into consumers' lives through our daily consumption.

While a growing number of companies profess to focus on modern slavery in their own operations and supply chains, there is a considerable gap between theory and practice. This is evident in the alarming number of modern slavery cases that continue to be exposed. The business narrative of aligning people, planet and profits is now commonplace, but is not always accompanied by meaningful action. In our view, too few companies are walking the talk. Even after the introduction of modern slavery laws in some countries, the fight against modern slavery remains largely dependent on corporate voluntarism and self-regulation.

Aside from modern slavery laws, international frameworks such as the United Nations Guiding Principles on Business and Human Rights and the Sustainable

Development Goals (SDGs) attempt to integrate human rights in business operations. Yet while formulated goals – such as the SDG's aim of eradicating modern slavery by 2030 – are praiseworthy, the uptake of these non-binding frameworks is patchy and progress is slow. As a society, we cannot afford to lazily rely on the coincidence between corporate goals and public interest to address modern slavery. Fortunately, there are several encouraging developments that can assist the fight against modern slavery. But first let us start with a deceptively simple question: what is modern slavery?

What's in a name?

Considering the dramatic increase in public interest over the past few years, it is remarkable that there is no globally recognised definition of modern slavery. Rather, modern slavery is an expression used by non-governmental organisations, intra-governmental organisations, governments, the media and other actors in the public domain to refer to a wide range of human rights abuses.[12]

Several exploitative practices are associated with modern slavery: forced labour, which refers to work that people must perform against their will under the threat of punishment; bonded or indebted labour, when individuals work to pay off a debt while losing control over working conditions and repayments; human trafficking, which concerns the recruitment and movement of people (usually for forced labour or sexual exploitation);

and child slavery, which is distinct from child labour as it involves not only children working but also their exploitation for someone else's gain. Other exploitative practices include deceptive recruitment for labour; domestic servitude; and forced marriage. Unlike the general term 'modern slavery', each of these the practices are crimes that do have individual definitions in national and international laws.[13]

The use of the term 'modern slavery' in public discourse and in this book constitutes a broad non-legal umbrella term that refers to a range of abusive practices. It is questionable, however, whether this expression constitutes a suitable overarching term. It is an emotive expression that conjures up images of historical slavery, thereby making the practice seem unrelated to present times. Furthermore, it paints a picture of exploiters and traffickers who need to be brought to justice and of victims who are waiting to be saved. It raises the notion of 'white saviour': the idea that the Westerners – white people, specifically – need to deliver civilisation to regions where modern slavery is rife, and free those who are exploited.

Such connotations incorrectly describe a complex issue, obscure our view of the true causes of exploitation, and deny agency to those exploited. Modern slavery also invokes images of the most shocking kinds of exploitation, thereby neglecting cases that are less likely to make headlines. Such flawed views of modern slavery may make it less likely that governments introduce appropriate legislation, while companies may not scrutinise their operations and supply chains, and consumers may not consider the social footprint of their purchases, as the existence of modern slavery remains beyond their comprehension.

Whether it is a suitable expression or not, the term 'modern slavery' has become commonplace in public discourse. Therefore, it is necessary to explain the workings at the core of this issue. Only then can public debate be well informed and effective interventions developed. A good starting point is to look at how slavery has evolved. The centuries old accounts of slavery throughout this chapter show that parallels and differences exist between historical and modern enslavement. Modern slavery should therefore not simply be seen as a continuation of an exploitative practice, but rather as an innovative response to abolition, providing new ways to carry out exploitation. Traditional slavery was enabled by institutions as it concerned the relationship between a master and a slave defined by legal ownership.[14] Since slavery has been officially abolished, enslavement no longer revolves around legal ownership, but around illegal control.

Two fundamental changes are the move away from the straightforward purchase of slave labour, and the existence of slaves as an employment category. While the statistics suggest that the 'market' for exploitative labour is booming, the notion that humans are purposefully sold and bought from an existing pool is outdated. While such basic transactions do still occur,[15] in contemporary cases people become trapped in slavery-like conditions in various ways. Understanding how this happens is of crucial importance if we are to bring modern slavery further into our realm of understanding.

Whether it concerns women tricked into sex work, men coerced to work in construction or agriculture, or children forced to work in mines or sweatshops, the term 'modern slavery' describes the lives and labour of individuals under the oppressive and illegal control of their exploiters, without alternatives available to them. The chains that hold humans today are more often psychological than they are physical.

How and where does modern slavery occur?

In our view, modern slavery should be seen as part of a continuum of exploitation. Such an outlook recognises that people can be exposed to working conditions that gradually worsen, sometimes leading to slavery or slavery-like conditions. Indeed, while some individuals 'enter labour situations that from the outset feature highly adverse conditions of little or no pay, debt or threats, [others] enter work on the expectation or promise of decent pay and conditions but find themselves in increasingly constrained and deteriorating circumstances that close down avenues for exit'.[16]

There are clear indicators of what makes workers more vulnerable to falling victim to modern slavery: limited language skills and knowledge of rights, gender (women are vastly overrepresented), migration status, and factors such as financial hardship or a history of unemployment. Many of the victims in the Australian cleaning industry (detailed below) are international students, whose visas limit their working hours to 40 hours per fortnight. This restriction makes workers vulnerable, because breaching visa conditions can result in (the threat of) being reported to the authorities by their employer. This gives unscrupulous employers the chance to exploit workers.

A large survey of migrants conducted in 2017 in Australia found that international students working more than 20 hours a week earn substantially lower wages than other students.[17] In 2015, two widely publicised media investigations found large-scale exploitation of migrant workers in Australia. The Australian television program *Four Corners* exposed widespread wage theft at 7-Eleven stores, where workers were systematically underpaid, and their complaints met with threats of deportation.[18] Together with Fairfax Media, *Four Corners* also revealed extensive underpayment and abuse of migrant workers in fresh-food supply chains, where groups of cut-price migrant workers were routinely offered to farms and factories by questionable labour-hire intermediaries.[19]

In a submission to the *Parliamentary Inquiry into*

Establishing a Modern Slavery Act in Australia, a former cleaner noted that exploitation in the cleaning industry is very common: 'Every [migrant] cleaner I know has been threatened, explicitly or implicitly, on the basis of their immigration status'.[20] For example, in 2017 a Sydney cleaning company that provided services to Bunnings, Wilson Parking and NSW Ambulance was fined AU$370 000 and ordered to back-pay AU$223 244 to 49 employees it had exploited. The Fair Work Ombudsman said that the matter 'involved dubious "labour hire" arrangements, corporate structures and sham contracting arrangements that were used … in a calculated attempt to avoid responsibility for vulnerable workers' entitlements'.[21] In the verdict, Justice Katzmann stated that many of the workers

> were foreign nationals on temporary visas, including student visas which restricted the number of hours during which they could work. Many had limited English language skills and were unlikely to have been familiar with Australian labour laws. Many, if not all, were struggling financially. Several had been unemployed for some time before securing work with the company. Some were treated by [the company] as slaves. 18 of the 49 employees in respect of whom compensation was sought were not paid anything for periods ranging from two weeks to two months.[22]

In 2018, the Australian Fair Work Ombudsman released the Harvest Trail Inquiry report, a five-year study detailing conditions experienced by seasonal harvest workers in Australia. Fair Work Inspectors completed 836 investigations, involving 444 growers and 194 labour-hire contractors. It recovered AU$1 022 698 for 2503 employees, but it believes the full extent of underpayments is significantly worse. Apart from widespread underpayment, the report found that workers were also exploited by other means. Labour-hire contractors commonly entered into agreements with ancillary service providers that were detrimental to workers, such as charging job-finding bonds; limiting accommodation options (which at times meant visa-holders had no work but accrued accommodation debts); offering overcrowded and substandard accommodation at above-market rates; and requiring workers to use specific transport providers while commuting.[23] All these actions are wilfully meant to exploit workers by limiting their options and charging excessive fees.

Less common, yet still occurring in wealthy countries, are cases where exploitation is accompanied by physical captivity. One example is the Filipino workers recruited to work in a massage shop in Canberra, the capital of Australia. Despite signing legal contracts, the employer confiscated workers' passports, and forced them to work 13.5 hours a day, six days a week, and pay back a substantial part of their earnings. They lived in overcrowded conditions, were kept under 24-hour guard, and were threatened with deportation, further wage deductions, and physical harm to them and their families if they spoke to authorities.[24]

Exploitation of workers that can be classified as modern slavery exists in many wealthy countries that we would not typically think to associate with it. Thousands of workers in hand car washes across Britain are believed to be victims of modern slavery. Investigations have found issues ranging from wage theft to human trafficking. In one case, trafficked individuals from eastern Europe were forced to work for two weeks and were paid £10; they relied on loose coins they found inside the cars to survive.[25] Despite their circumstances, many choose not to contact authorities fearing they would be seen as illegal immigrants.[26] In 2019, the British government rejected proposals to force car-wash owners to apply for licences, in favour of endorsing a voluntary, industry-led scheme recognising good practice.[27]

Similarly, one does not have to travel to Thailand to witness modern slavery in the fishing industry: migrant workers on Irish and British trawlers have experienced exploitation, physical abuse and underpayment. A majority of the men interviewed on Irish vessels worked more than 100 hours a week for an average pay of just under €3 per hour,[28] while several African and Asian crew members on British trawlers were identified as victims of modern slavery.[29] A permit scheme for fishing workers from outside the European Economic Area allowed boat owners to legally acquire visas for hundreds of foreign crew members who had previously been brought in and employed illegally as cheap labour. However, the scheme tied workers to individual employers, leaving many vulnerable to abusive conditions and in fear of deportation if they complained or wanted to leave. Boat owners also deducted the typical fee of €1000 for permits from their wages. Some trawler companies were paying a fraction of the legal minimum wage and were regularly requiring migrants to work dangerously long hours without sleep, resulting in repeated cases of industrial injury.[30] In 2018, Ireland was downgraded by the United States' State Department in its annual report on countries' efforts to fight trafficking. In 2019, Ireland came to an agreement with the International Transport Workers' Federation – a trade union – to grant migrant workers on Irish fishing ships additional protections.[31]

All these scenarios describe modern slavery and illustrate that this practice can take different forms. It becomes clear that exploitation does not always have to be premeditated or involve human trafficking and captivity. Rather, the scenarios illustrate the continuum of labour exploitation, the deterioration of labour standards, and the absence of legal recourse that results in workers being at the mercy of their employers, leaving them no other option than to do as they are told. The examples of exploitation in the cleaning industry, at 7-Eleven and in the horticultural sector show that, despite falling victim to modern slavery, individuals may still be paid (reduced) wages.

AGRICULTURAL SLAVERY

For it is a common practice ... for men to purchase slaves though they have not plantations themselves, in order to let them out to planters and merchants at so much a piece by the day, and they give what allowance they chuse out of this produce of their daily work to their slaves for subsistence; this allowance is often very scanty. My master often gave the owners of these slaves two and a half of these pieces per day, and found the poor fellows in victuals himself, because he thought their owners did not feed them well enough according to the work they did.

Olaudah Equiano (1789).[32]

A recruiter came to our village, people were asked to gather round, and we were told about working in America and how much we would earn. $20 000 US dollar is a lot of money. It would be impossible for me to earn that much in Thailand, but it was necessary since I wanted to build a future for my family. I had to get a bank loan of around $22 000 in total. We were told our food bills and other expenses would be deducted from our pay. After we arrived, they said they couldn't pay what was promised. We got paid less than the amount deducted for the food bills. We had to live in a container without running water with more than 20 people. Living like this made me want to go home, but I couldn't because I had a huge debt.

Thanit, Thailand (2011).[33]

The distinctive feature in all cases is the abusive control exercised by employers, who by means of threats, coercion or manipulation dictate exploitative working conditions while limiting workers' alternatives. Crucially, any of the victims in these scenarios may be perceived as having a 'normal job'. Consumers getting a coffee at the convenience store, someone getting a remedial massage, companies outsourcing their office cleaning, or a shopper buying fruit at the supermarket: one could quite easily not give a second thought to the working conditions of the people producing these goods or offering these services.

These cases illustrate that contemporary exploiters are not just modern-day equivalents of traditional plantation owners. Although modern slavery is prevalent in the agricultural sector, and while exploitation does occur in some industries more than in others,[34] it is certainly not limited to particular sectors. Modern slavery can occur wherever people are prepared to illegitimately control and exploit vulnerable individuals for financial gain. Moreover, exploiters should not be regarded as a uniform group. As is illustrated by the cases, modern slavery may be deliberately orchestrated, and involve the transport and false imprisonment of people; in other instances, illegal control is the result of people's misfortune or hardship being opportunistically taken advantage of by employers.

Rather than occurring purely in parallel to the formal economy, modern-slavery practices in the so-called shadow economy are frequently linked to the legitimate market for goods and services. There is, therefore, no escaping the reality that modern slavery is a pervasive feature of the global economy. As will be shown in chapter 2, employment relationships are becoming increasingly fractured.[35] This means that companies may benefit from modern slavery through the outsourcing of production, without being directly involved in these activities. This exposes companies to the risk of profiting from exploitation, and links consumers and governments to modern slavery through individual purchases and public procurement.[36]

Modern slavery in its various forms is, therefore, not an abnormality confined to the fringes of society and the dark corners of the economy, or something that takes place only in impoverished regions and countries, solely perpetuated by shadowy figures – it is connected to all of us. The global profits of modern slavery are substantial. Based on an estimate of 21 million people in modern slavery around the world in 2012, the International Labour Organization approximated that US$150 billion in illegal profits are generated in the private economy each year.[37] It has been calculated that the average profit per victim is US$3978 per year.[38] Given that the latest estimation of people in modern slavery has nearly doubled, associated profits will have drastically risen as well.

Why has modern slavery thrived?

A holistic perspective is necessary in order to fully comprehend why modern slavery has thrived. Any examination of modern slavery should observe the broader socio-economic context in which exploitation takes place and include an analysis of the local circumstances in which people are abused. Large-scale factors that need to be considered include issues such as economic globalisation, income inequality, migration trends and labour rights. At the local level, poverty and unsustainable debt, as well as voluntary or involuntary displacement leave people highly vulnerable to labour exploitation.

Although all these issues are highly important, they are by no means part of an exhaustive list. Any large- or small-scale factor that undermines a person's capacity to make an autonomous decision about their own working life can result in exploitation. Modern slavery can, therefore, arise at any time and in any place where people are willing to trick or coerce vulnerable people into exploitative working conditions without viable alternatives.

In order to explain the existence of 40.3 million people in modern slavery around the world, we need to discuss economic globalisation. The growth of free trade in recent decades has been heralded for stimulating economic development and criticised for increasing inequality. While the world economy has indeed grown, not everyone has benefited from this development. Although many have been lifted out of poverty, around

736 million people continue to live in extreme poverty, earning less than US$1.90 per day.[39] People living in poverty struggle to meet basic needs, and as well as lacking economic resources, they often do not have any social and political capital. These destitute groups and individuals are at greater risk of falling victim to modern slavery.[40]

In his bestselling book *Capital in the 21st Century*, economist Thomas Piketty explains that while the global economy is larger than it has ever been, wealth is less evenly shared – both within countries and between regions.[41] Wage growth across the world has lagged behind the growth of labour productivity in recent decades, which means that the wage share of national income, or the sum of income given to a country's inhabitants each year, has been in decline.[42] In Australia in early 2017, the wage share of national income hit its lowest level since 1959.[43] The decline in wage share around the world has coincided with a global increase in inequality, including in two-thirds of countries belonging to the Organisation for Economic Co-operation and Development (OECD) countries as well as in some of the large emerging economies.[44]

Being paid a wage does not mean escaping poverty, as workers at the lower end of the labour market often remain in debt and struggle to feed their families. The charitable organisation Oxfam estimated that the richest 1 per cent of people are now as wealthy as the rest of the world combined.[45] It also calculated that it takes a CEO from one of the top five global fashion brands only four days to earn what a Bangladeshi garment worker earns in their entire lifetime, and that in 2017, 82 per cent of all of the growth in global wealth went to the top 1 per cent, whereas the bottom 50 per cent saw no increase at all.[46] Clearly, the global economy is built on the backs of low-paid and exploited workers.

Economic globalisation is an asymmetrical process that favours some countries, regions, cities and groups while excluding others.[47] Early and positive views on globalisation included that the world had 'flattened' and that opportunity structures had become more egalitarian.[48] Considering the increase in income inequality between and within countries, the reverse seems to have happened: globalisation has benefited some, rather than having levelled the playing field for all.

The unequal economic outcomes of globalisation are prominently reflected in migration patterns. Rather than witnessing a global increase in the volume and diversity of migration, shifts in migration have been one-directional and are linked to skewed economic development. Migration from poor countries to a select number of destination countries has increased.[49] The potential for these migrants to benefit from globalisation is hindered by restrictive policies in the destination countries, which frequently favour giving employment, residence and protective labour rights to skilled and rich migrants while excluding lower-skilled and poorer migrants.[50]

For example, to suit labour market needs, the

Australian migration balance moved from family migration towards skilled migration. Family migration made up two-thirds and skilled migration one-third of permanent resettlement in 1996 – in 2017 these ratios were reversed. There has also been a large increase in temporary migration to Australia through short-term work visas.[51] As mentioned earlier, high-profile cases of migrant-worker exploitation in Australia, including labour exploitation of temporary migrants in the horticultural sector, have been the subject of significant media attention.[52]

Wage theft is widespread among temporary migrants: a 2017 survey of 4322 temporary migrants from 107 countries found that one in three international students and backpackers in Australia were paid about half the legal minimum wage.[53] The International Organization for Migration notes that 'migrant workers around the world generally lack the legal protection available to the domestic workforce', and that 'irregular migrant workers are particularly vulnerable to exploitation and abuses in the workplace, including slavery-like practices'.[54] Tellingly, while both the UK and Australia have introduced modern anti-slavery laws, neither country is party to the International Convention on the Protection of the Rights of All Migrant Workers and Members of their Families, one of the core United Nations (UN) human rights treaties.[55]

The risk of falling victim to exploitation and modern slavery is not only determined by economic indicators

CAPTIVITY AND ABUSE

Being in this dreadful captivity and horrible slavery, without any hope of deliverance, for about eight or nine months, beholding the most dreadful scenes of misery and cruelty, and seeing my miserable companions often cruelly lashed, and, as it were, cut to pieces, for the most trifling faults; this made me often tremble and weep, but I escaped better than many ...

Ottobah Cugoano (1787).[56]

We sailed for days and days before they told us we'd been sold to the Thais to work as fishermen. I went to the captain and complained. He beat me so badly, it was impossible for me to work, eat or sleep. I thought I was going to die. We sailed until we were in Indonesian waters. The days turned into weeks and the weeks into months. My health, and the beatings, got worse.'

Yum, Cambodia, (2017).[57]

but is then aggravated by a lack of rights and social protections. Early studies suggested that the efforts by emerging and export-oriented countries to attract foreign direct investment are linked to weakening of labour provisions[58], and a recent study shows that labour standards provisions in free trade agreements are characterised by a 'lack of legal and political prioritization'.[59] The role of free trade in enabling economic development is therefore paradoxical: although it can create jobs, stimulate growth and improve people's livelihoods, profits are often the result of dubious labour standards where rights and protections are lacking.

While advocates of economic globalisation contend that free trade has increased overall economic welfare, critics argue that the relentless search for low-cost goods and services has caused a global 'race to the bottom': production is relocated to areas where labour is cheapest, which are often regions where labour regulation is weak or hardly enforced.[60] An early and well-documented example of the link between globalisation and poor labour standards concerns Nike, whose apparel was found to have been produced in sweatshops since the 1970s.[61] Despite the emergence of private governance initiated by companies in response to labour exploitation, stories about labour abuses remain commonplace. Many producing and export-oriented countries have not experienced an improvement of labour standards.[62]

The decline in rights and social protections has not only affected migrant workers in developed countries and workers in export-oriented countries. The liberalising of labour markets has also been accompanied by the dismantling of social institutions in many affluent countries, where reforms have promoted labour flexibility and weakened domestic workers' bargaining power.[63] As a result, fewer people enjoy job security and non-wage benefits, while there has been an increase in unstable work without non-wage benefits and labour rights.[64]

The crucial factor to consider in this context is the shift in risk from employers to workers: rather than companies having to worry about having too many permanent employees on the payroll, workers need to worry about job security. The link between precarious work and the ability to exercise labour rights is key to understanding how worsening working conditions can lead to modern slavery.[65] Flexibility in the labour market is often promoted as providing workers with the freedom to choose, yet for many people accepting precarious work with limited rights is a question of survival. With workers reluctant to complain out of fear of losing their jobs, and with limited avenues for remedy, this creates a situation where exploitative employers can act with impunity.

The late sociologist Pierre Bourdieu was an early and vocal critic of economic globalisation. He branded it as 'fake universalism', which 'serves in reality the interest of the dominant [and] leaves citizens isolated and disarmed in the face of the overwhelming power of transnational corporations'.[66] Bourdieu coined the term 'flexploitation' to describe the increasing casualisation of work.[67] More recently, this growing group at the lower end of labour markets has been labelled the 'precariat': those who live in economic uncertainty, with unstable earnings and unsustainable debt, on the brink of destitution.[68]

In Europe, the US and other affluent countries, an increasing number of people are classified as 'the working poor' and are unable to make ends meet through employment.[69] Manuel Castells, a well-known theorist of globalisation, argues that a 'new geography of social exclusion' has emerged that he calls the 'fourth world', which 'comprises large areas of the globe, such as much of Sub-Saharan Africa, and the impoverished rural areas of Latin America and Asia. But it is also present in literally every country, and every city'.[70] Whether they are called the precariat or inhabitants of the fourth world, these people have found themselves on the wrong side of economic globalisation.

The most serious threat from economic globalisation to working and living standards, however, is not posed by trade or investment, which can at least, in theory, improve the livelihoods of more than just a select few, but is the withdrawal of the state as the guardian of the public interest. In recent decades, the capitalist mode of production in its various forms, premised on the accumulation of wealth through private rather than public ownership, has been the driving force of the world economy.

Where capitalism is the economic operating model of globalisation, neoliberalism is its facilitating public policy approach. While differences between countries exist, the consensus among policymakers is that a largely unregulated free market economy achieves the best outcomes for society. Governments, thus, have a reduced role and little appetite to intervene in markets or to correct corporate behaviour, despite the dire social consequences. In the words of Bernie Fraser, former governor of the Reserve Bank of Australia, neoliberalism '[favours] the market system ahead of the state system, and individual interests ahead of community interests, [which] can lead to profoundly unfair social outcomes'.[71]

Modern slavery is everywhere

Illustrations of modern slavery can demonstrate the link between economic globalisation, growing inequality, migration and a lack of rights, and show how these factors have given rise to structural exploitation around the world. For example, measured in per capita income, Qatar has become the richest country in the world.[72] The emirate has experienced a construction boom worth around US$220 billion, partly driven by preparations for hosting the FIFA World Cup in 2022.[73] This boom has attracted significant foreign investment, as well as an incredible number of migrant workers from impoverished regions, who make up more than 90 per cent of Qatar's population of 2.1 million.[74]

Yet several investigations reveal that migrants are systematically exploited and marginalised. Security guards, hospitality workers and gardeners, hired via deceptive recruitment agents to work in the rapidly growing number of hotels, are overworked, underpaid and live in labour camps.[75] The International Trade Union Confederation estimates that more than 1200 migrant workers have died in Qatar in recent years, some while constructing World Cup facilities. It predicts that there will be at least 4000 more fatalities by the time the World Cup commences – a figure disputed by the Qatari authorities.[76] Amnesty International found that passport confiscation, delayed wage payments and deceptive recruitment are widespread. It also notes that many migrant workers are indebted, having taken out loans to pay fees to the labour supply companies that sponsored them to come to Qatar.[77] A migrant worker who spoke to Amnesty International said:

> My life here is like a prison. The work is difficult, we worked for many hours in the hot sun. When I first complained about my situation, soon after arriving in Qatar, the manager said, 'If you want to complain you can, but there will be consequences. If you want to stay in Qatar, be quiet and keep working.' Now I am forced to stay in Qatar and continue working.[78]

Until recently, under Qatar's kafala system, the nearly two million migrant workers could not leave their jobs or the country without their sponsors' permission. Kafala systems exist in various forms across the Middle East. These sponsorship systems are used to monitor migrant labourers.

Qatari authorities have introduced reforms, but workers are still unable to change employers without permission from their initial sponsor. The changes exclude migrants not under the labour law, such as those in the military, public sector and domestic work; employers can also apply to exclude other workers.[79] In Qatar, migrant workers are routinely marginalised: various markets, shopping malls and town squares have been euphemistically designated as 'family zones' and are only accessible for locals and Westerners. Armed security guards bar those suspected of being migrant workers from entry.[80]

While Qatar needs to import workers, several countries in Asia – such as Cambodia – are experiencing a labour surplus. Regional worker shortages and labour surpluses do not only create cross-border flows of migrant workers, they can also cause displacement of people within countries.[81] Like Qatar, Cambodia's capital, Phnom Penh, is experiencing a construction boom, partly fuelled by foreign investment and lauded by the World Bank.[82] While Cambodia is one of Asia's fastest growing economies, inequality is staggering: a two-bedroom apartment in the capital costs more than 200 times the average annual wage.[83]

Disturbingly, the bricks used in the construction of new buildings in Cambodia are produced by tens of thousands of debt-bonded families. Unseasonal rains and drought caused by climate change have pushed many farmers into unsustainable debt, often with one of the country's unregulated microfinance bodies. Indebted and with few non-farm job prospects, brick-kiln owners will pay creditors if entire families move and work in the kilns until debts are repaid. Adults and children are exposed to noxious gases and dangerous working conditions; limbs are amputated regularly due to dangerous machinery. Workers are unable to leave even in the off-season and many remain there for decades.[84]

In the case of debt-bonded Cambodian families working in brick kilns, the 'race to the bottom' seems to have become something else entirely. Their predicament is not the result of labour costs and labour standards plummeting to the lowest possible point. Instead, the existence of surplus labour,[85] in combination with unsustainable debt and a lack of social protection offered by the Cambodian state, has transformed cheap labour into indebted labour. Everything that these Cambodian farmers working as brick producers possess, including their future income, has become beholden to their creditors. Former farmers, therefore, no longer simply present 'value' through their labour but also through their debts.[86] They are displaced, powerless and at the mercy of their employer-creditor. In an economic model such as this, protecting labour standards and enforcing

DOMESTIC SERVITUDE

The next morning my mistress set about instructing me in my tasks. She taught me to do all sorts of household work; to wash and bake, pick cotton and wool, and wash floors, and cook. And she taught me (how can I ever forget it!) more things than these; she caused me to know the exact difference between the smart of the rope, the cart-whip, and the cow-skin, when applied to my naked body by her own cruel hand. And there was scarcely any punishment more dreadful than the blows received on my face and head from her hard-heavy fist. She was a fearful woman, and a savage mistress to her slaves.

Mary Prince (1831).[87]

My chores seem unending. I wash the windows, walls and bathrooms. I shampoo carpets, polish floors and clean furniture. After 20 hours I am still not done. There's no food on my plate for dinner, so I scavenge through the trash. I try to call the job agency, but the woman who now owns me has locked the telephone. I try to flee the apartment, but she has locked the door. I can feel the burning on my cheeks as she slaps me. It is night and her kids have gone to sleep. Grasping me by the hair, she bangs my head into the wall and throws me to the floor. She kicks me and hits me with a broom. If I scream or fight back, she will kill me. So, I bite my lips to bare the pain and then I pass out. This is my daily routine, the life of a slave.

Beatrice, Sri Lanka, (2013).[88]

rights alone will not make a difference. Rather, microfinance markets need to be regulated to avoid debt traps, while the state needs to address displacement and poverty resulting from climate change.[89]

Modern slavery is also rife in the agricultural industry. Commonly cited examples include cocoa, coffee, palm oil and sugar cane, which are mostly cultivated in Africa, South America and Asia. Yet exploitation is not limited to these crops or these regions. In the Italian agricultural sector, the gangmaster system – recruitment of labour on behalf of third parties under exploitative conditions – is common: vulnerable migrants are organised into groups that are then hired to harvest crops. While workers make around €30 a day, they are forced to pay up to half their income to cover transport costs, food, water and a cut to the gangmaster. Court documents show that victims worked for 12 hours a day, seven days a week, without breaks and for little reward.[90]

In Spain, migrants working on tomato, pepper, cucumber and courgette farms have also fallen victim to modern slavery. Conditions worsened after the Spanish property boom collapsed, which drove thousands of migrants – many undocumented – from construction into horticulture. Migrants were found living in dwellings made of boxes and plastic sheeting, which lacked sanitation and drinking water, and being paid less than half the minimum wage. Workers without papers were threatened they would be reported if they complained.[91] Since the start of the migrant crisis in

2015, hundreds of thousands of economic migrants and asylum seekers have crossed the Mediterranean destined for Europe and are at great risk of exploitation.[92]

Modern slavery affects us all

To comprehend the workings of modern slavery, it is necessary to have both an informed public debate and to formulate effective interventions. Unfortunately, victims are often described as illegal workers rather than victims of modern slavery, both by the media and by politicians.[93] This occurs even in the UK and Australia, which have both introduced modern-slavery legislation. This illustrates a lack of compassion as well as a lack of understanding of the core dynamics of modern slavery.

A woman who was trafficked to Britain at the age of three and sexually exploited for decades was told by the Home Office that she resided in the UK illegally, even though she did not even know where she was trafficked from. Several Chinese women who were trafficked to Britain were sent to detention without legal representation or access to medical care. A man who was sold into slavery at the age of three in Ghana, and was then trafficked to the UK, was told by authorities he would be deported back to the country where all he knew were his captors. It took the Court of Appeal to stop it.[94]

In Australia, the former federal immigration minister Peter Dutton said in response to modern slavery in the horticulture industry: 'I don't want Australians being displaced from work by foreign workers … If we have foreign workers here I don't want them being exploited by labour hire companies or other employers'.[95]

To date, documented cases of modern slavery in wealthier countries have often involved migrants, who are more vulnerable to exploitation, due to their legal status. Yet the rise of wage theft, insecure work, unsustainable household debt and poverty trends[96] make the scenario of exploited citizens and residents an increasingly realistic prospect. Modern slavery never occurs in isolation. It needs to be seen in the context of broader social and economic developments. Failure to consider the underlying factors that lead to exploitation results in an incomplete understanding of modern slavery and reduces the likelihood that effective legislation and corporate policies will be implemented. It also reduces the prospect of consumers understanding how they are linked to forced labour. It is crucial to realise that everyone has a slavery footprint, depending on your lifestyle, and what you own, wear and eat.

The organisation 'Made in a Free World' created an online tool to demonstrate how much of our day-to-day lives involve slavery through global supply chains.[97] It estimates that someone living in Seattle, USA, who has one child with some toys, a furnished rental home, a car, an average diet, wardrobe and range of toiletries, as well as mobile phone and other electronics, has about 73 slaves working for them worldwide. Modern slavery happens everywhere and is directly linked to companies, governments and consumers. Whether you are a holiday-maker in Qatar or attending the World Cup in 2022, a company importing bricks from or investing in the Cambodian property boom, a consumer getting your car washed or buying scallops in the UK, or a large supermarket sourcing fresh produce in Italy, Spain or Australia, you are likely profiting from modern slavery.

2

Global supply chains: Pervasive and intractable

Global supply chains affect every aspect of our lives. Your car has parts that were produced in and sourced from different regions, before it was (partly) assembled in one or more low-wage countries and shipped to its destination country.[1] The mineral mica, which is used to add a shimmer to car paint, has been linked to child and forced labour.[2] In fact, it has been revealed that the deaths of several children in illegal mines in India were covered up to avoid damaging the mica industry. Manufacturers such as Volkswagen and Mercedes-Benz have announced a review of their mica supply chains.[3] Pig iron, an ingredient of steel and cast iron also used in car manufacturing, is often sourced from Brazil, where it has been found that blast furnaces are operated by means of slave labour.[4] Greenpeace found that carmakers Ford, General Motors, BMW, Mercedes-Benz and Nissan are connected to companies that source from Brazil.[5]

If you get your car polished at a car wash you may also be benefiting from modern slavery.[6] The shipping company that brought your car (parts) to its destination country may have removed its domestic crew to reduce labour costs.[7] Many ships sail under the flag of a country other than the country of ownership. This allows owners to take advantage of minimal regulation and low registration fees, to avoid taxes and to source labour from anywhere.[8] In 2017, an abandoned crew was found in the UK without access to potable water and eating out-of-date food. The crew had not been paid for months; many had not received any wages since joining the vessel a year earlier, and some even had to pay to get their jobs.[9]

It is hard to overstate the impact of global supply chains on the economy and people's lives. The Organisation for Economic Co-operation and Development (OECD) estimates that more than half of the world's manufactured imports are intermediate goods, which are used in the production of other goods.[10] Trade, production, investment, employment relations and labour itself have drastically changed with the growth of supply chains. The United Nations Conference on Trade and Development estimates that approximately 80 per cent of international trade can now be linked to the global production networks of multinational enterprises.[11]

In the 40 countries that make up 85 per cent of the global gross domestic product, and account for around two-thirds of the labour force around the world, employment linked to supply chains has increased by 53 per cent since 1995, culminating in 453 million formal jobs in supply chains in 2013.[12] The International Trade Union Confederation estimates that 60 per cent of global trade in the real economy depends on the supply chains of 50 corporations, which employ only 6 per cent of workers directly but rely on a hidden workforce of 116 million people.[13] Crucially, companies that source through supply chains do not have responsibilities to workers at suppliers and subcontractors in the same way as they do to their own employees.

These facts demonstrate the growing influence of global supply chains, the international fragmentation of production, the changing nature of employment relations, the unprecedented power of a few large corporations, and the extent of labour exploitation around the world. Together, these factors raise several challenges. While many companies have seized the economic opportunities in burgeoning markets – arguably while creating local jobs and contributing to regional economic prosperity – the custom to outsource production and source from low-cost regions creates an opaque network of global suppliers.

This mode of production generates immense cost pressures that are passed on to suppliers. The handful of supermarket giants that dominate global food sales are a prime example. Just four companies – Archer Daniels Midland, Bunge, Cargill and the Louis Dreyfus Company (known as the 'ABCD group') – account for 70 per cent of trade in commodities such as wheat, corn and soybeans; in addition, only 50 companies account for half of all global food sales.[14] Their grip on the market and on supply chains has resulted in low prices, yet their enormous buying power exerts continual pressure on suppliers to cut costs.[15] Labour is an area of production in which savings can be made easily by cutting corners. Various forms of labour exploitation are the true price that is paid for this reduction in labour costs.[16] Cost pressures and unscrupulous sourcing can result in companies being ignorant or wilfully disregarding their social responsibilities, while creating situations in which both companies and consumers are linked to labour and human rights abuses.

It is beyond doubt that the rise of global sourcing and production has had negative side effects, and that business innovation has not been without undesirable consequences.[17] New production regimes associated with supply chains such as just-in-time production and lean manufacturing, which respectively require suppliers to ensure speedy and timely delivery and produce at maximum capacity with minimum means (of labour), often generate non-standard and precarious forms of employment.[18] Due to the increased flexibility of labour in supply chains and the relentless search for cheap labour, many (low-skilled) jobs disappear as abruptly as they appeared. Once production or sourcing becomes cheaper elsewhere, there is nothing to stop a lead company from switching suppliers or moving production, leaving many without the means to make a living. Local suppliers will often attempt to deal with this threat by cutting labour costs even further.[19]

In supply chains, a sudden increase in demand for a particular commodity can also lead to exploitation. An example is the previously discussed mica, a mineral used in paints but also in cosmetic products. The global craze for cosmetics with 'natural minerals' has sent illegal operators rushing to the hundreds of decommissioned mines in India and has created a lucrative black market: 70 per cent of mica production in India is from illegal mining associated with child labour and debt bondage.[20] Production and sourcing through global supply chains, therefore, not only potentially undermine labour standards, they can also generate activity in the informal and black economy.

The dark side of development

The practice of using slave labour has adapted to changes in the political and economic landscape. As mentioned in chapter 1, slavery is no longer defined by legal ownership but by illegal control. Whether modern slavery is planned and organised by traffickers, or arises as a result of opportunism among employers, a range of innovative practices can be identified in the 'business model' of modern slavery.[21] Traffickers take on a new role as intermediaries by illegally transporting people for the sake of profiting from their labour, benefiting from poverty, inequality and restrictive immigration policies. The undocumented status of trafficked individuals makes them highly vulnerable to exploitation, a fact that is knowingly exploited. Even if workers have migrated through official channels, a frequent lack of knowledge regarding language and labour rights is routinely preyed upon.

The practices of some labour hire companies, which benefit from the outsourcing and subcontracting by companies seeking to cut labour costs, are examples of exploitation linked to supply chains. Many dubious labour intermediaries evade legal requirements regarding wages, working conditions, benefits and taxes by underpaying workers, forcing excessive overtime, confiscating identity documents and threatening workers with deportation.

Economic globalisation and business innovation have outpaced the development of internationally binding norms concerning corporate responsibility for labour standards and human rights. This is a key issue. The environment in which governance arrangements are established is patchy, due to the increase in cross-border sourcing and production, trade liberalisation and the deregulation of labour markets. Existing labour regulation has a national scope, meaning that companies operating directly in host countries have to consider regulations that are different from those in their home country. Consequently, the governance of labour standards and the protection of human rights in global supply chains is characterised by a mix of jurisdictions, norms and actors, while approaches differ depending on national, industry and company factors. These complications are described as governance and enforcement gaps.[22] Initiatives to bridge these gaps range from international framework agreements that mimic collective bargaining to market-based initiatives that produce voluntary standards.[23]

Despite ongoing discussions at the United Nations (UN) about a binding treaty on business and human rights, progress has been slow. In the absence of political will among governments,[24] approaches to labour and human rights abuses continue to build on the existing legal frameworks of nation-states with some influence from non-binding international guidelines, as discussed in chapter 1. Even in cases where legislation has been passed with specific regard to modern slavery, such as in the UK and Australia, requirements imposed on companies are limited to annual reports on the risks of modern slavery in their operations and supply chains, the actions taken to assess and address those risks, and the effectiveness of these responses. Furthermore, the laws are seen to lack 'teeth' due to the lack of enforcement mechanisms and penalties for non-compliance.

Due to the prevalence of neoliberal policies and the hesitancy of states to intervene in business affairs and markets, approaches to combat modern slavery rely heavily on the self-regulatory capacity of companies. That is, voluntary efforts of a company to avoid and mitigate social and environmental transgressions in their operations and supply chains. This creates a paradoxical situation: the companies that benefit from cheap labour and poor labour standards are relied upon to improve working conditions and protect rights. This regulatory approach assumes that companies are ready and willing to undermine a business model from which they profit in order to protect the rights of workers.

Stories about modern slavery remain commonplace, despite a host of corporate social responsibility and private governance initiatives that have been developed in response to corporate labour and human rights violations. It seems that relying on the coincidence between corporate goals and public interest, mediated by market mechanisms instead of legal frameworks, does not automatically lead to a structural improvement of labour standards and observance of human rights by companies.

Corporate stakeholders such as (institutional) investors and consumers have not yet lost faith in the capacity of companies to self-regulate and take voluntary measures. This is due, in part, to the ability of companies to effectively manage negativity surrounding their activities, and the capacity to neutralise reputational threats to the company by taking symbolic rather than substantive action. Electronics giant Apple is a good example: despite introducing codes of conduct and auditing their suppliers, the company has experienced a decade of continuing human rights abuses in its supply chain, yet Apple's financial success indicates it has not suffered any reputational damage as a result.[25]

High-risk industries

The number of industries, goods and services that are associated with modern slavery is staggering. Every two years the United States Department of Labor produces a list of goods produced by child or forced labour. In 2018, this list comprised a total of 148 goods from 76 countries. The goods with the most mentions of forced labour by number of countries are bricks, cotton, garments, cattle and sugar cane.[26] Notorious industries include the manufacturing, mining and agricultural sectors. The International Labour Organization (ILO) estimated that in 2017, the agricultural sector contained more than 1.1 million victims.[27]

There are several reasons why workers in the agricultural sector are prone to falling victim to modern slavery. Work in this industry often has a low barrier of entry, meaning that few skills are required to gain employment, a factor that can lead to child labour and attracts people who have few alternative employment prospects available to them. In many countries that rely on agricultural exports, minimum wages do not exist or are far below a living wage.[28] In addition, agricultural labour frequently involves seasonal or temporary work,

MODERN SLAVERY IN AGRICULTURE

Australia's 'Seasonal Worker Program' initiative aims to provide foreign aid to participating countries through seasonal work opportunities for their citizens. Although there are a range of minimum requirements in place and the usual protections of Australian workplace laws, there have been many instances of exploitation of seasonal farm workers.

Maroochy Sunshine Pty Ltd was a labour-hire company controlled by its sole director Mr Emmanuel Bani in southeast Queensland.[29] In 2014, Mr. Bani promoted the program in Vanuatu and recruited 22 citizens for the fruit-picking season with a contract that stated an hourly wage of AU$16. Although Mr Bani collected the earnings from their labour, more than half the workers were not paid at all for the entire duration of their stay and the remainder were paid AU$150 in cash for the cumulative six months of work. When they asked for their wages, Mr Bani threatened to call the police.[30] The workers often would only eat one meal a day that consisted of half a sandwich or pumpkins or potatoes. There were entire days when the workers were given no food and were forced to sleep on the side of the road or in buses.[31] The judgement of the Federal Circuit Court Case that indicted Mr Bani and his company noted that the physical, economic and mental impact of the bonded labour stayed with the workers even after they returned to Vanuatu.[32] Many of them were unable to repay the loans they had taken to fund the seasonal work opportunity, while others felt embarrassed to return to Vanuatu without the promised income to support their families.[33]

which attracts migrant workers, and much of the work is quota based, leaving workers vulnerable to wage theft.

Agricultural sites are often in remote locations, whether it concerns tea pickers on isolated estates, labourers on remote cocoa farms, or a crew on a fishing trawler. Such workers are harder for authorities, trade unions, civil society organisations and supply chain auditors to reach than those people who work in metropolitan areas or in factories. This adds to their vulnerability and increases the possibility of falling victim to modern slavery.[34] The lack of visibility of human rights abuses is exacerbated by ever lengthening supply chains, and the spread of industries into remote areas; for example, through land clearing for cattle ranches in the Amazon,[35] land grabs for natural resources,[36] and fishing the seas in South-East Asia.[37]

One country with a high risk for agricultural slavery is Thailand. Thousands of migrants come to Thailand each year, a country that is a point of origin, transit hub and destination for many slaves.[38] Many have been and many still are sold into slavery and are forced to work on fishing boats – often for years on end and under threat of violence and death.[39] Through supply chains that include 'middle men', subsidiaries and multinationals, seafood caught and processed through the use of forced labour is sold to American, European and Australian consumers by global retailers. While government reforms and private initiatives have been launched in Thailand and Indonesia, trafficking and forced labour continue. Human Rights Watch describes the reforms and inspection regimes as a 'theatrical exercise for international consumption'.[40]

In 2015, despite inspecting 474334 fishing crew, Thai authorities did not find a single case of forced labour.[41] To show that these findings do not reflect the actual situation in the Thai fishing industry, Human Rights Watch conducted interviews over the course of two years with nearly 250 fisherman, officials, boat owners, activists and UN staff working in major Thai fishing ports. It details how – four years after the revelations of slavery aboard fishing boats in Thailand – migrants continue to be trafficked and sold to work on fishing boats for no pay or little pay, and without the option to leave or change employer.[42] An industry body called the Sustainable Seafood Taskforce, consisting of supermarkets, buyers and retailers, was created in 2015 to tackle slavery in the Thai seafood industry. According to a non-governmental organisation that has worked with Thai authorities to achieve reforms, the Sustainable Seafood Taskforce is 'more focused on talking in hotel rooms in Bangkok rather than actually committing to using their influence to create real change'.[43]

Modern slavery also occurs in the largest consumer markets in the world. An Al-Jazeera documentary detailed how an American recruitment company, Global Horizons, came to Thailand searching for workers.[44] People in rural villages are an easy target for recruiters,

SLAVERY AT SEA

For several years, Thailand's fishing industry has come under scrutiny for forced labour and other human rights abuses. It is often migrant workers who are affected as they form a significant proportion of the workforce. Thailand's Department of Fisheries has noted that 82 per cent of workers were from neighbouring countries such as Cambodia, Laos and Myanmar.[45]

At 57 years old, Saw Win was one such Burmese migrant who arrived in Thailand in 2011 after being promised by a broker that he would be transported across the border for a job that paid US$4.50 a day.[46] Looking forward to the opportunity to support his family back home, Saw Win agreed to be taken to the port town of Kantang in Thailand – a journey that, despite the broker's promises of safety, involved being covered in a tarpaulin and suffocating in the cargo bed of a truck. Upon arrival, Saw Win was sold to one of the many brokers who managed migrant workers at the town's fishing piers.

From this point, Saw Win suffered detention, significant abuse and enslavement for many years, with most of his time forcibly spent on the fishing vessel. He received no pay for any of his work and was compensated only with meagre amounts of food at the discretion of the skipper. When his boat returned to the port every few months, he was locked in a room with 40 other men until they were assigned to other boats. He witnessed the physical abuse and even killing of his fellow workers when he was forced to spend one year fishing illegally in the South China Sea.[47] This was not a rare occurrence as a study by the United Nations Inter-Agency Project on Human Trafficking (UNIAP) found that almost 59 per cent of migrant workers in the Thai fishing industry had witnessed the killing of a crew member.[48] Seafood from Thailand is exported by global companies to supermarkets in Australia, the US and Europe.

who make promises about a better life in America. Workers had to pay recruitment and registration fees in advance. These fees were higher than the maximum allowed under foreign worker programs, and many workers took out loans from banks or loan sharks. As a result, they became heavily indebted and had no choice but to work to pay off their debts. Many ended up working on large farms in the US that supply to the world's largest food companies. Upon arrival, their passports were taken by their employers.

They were told their food and accommodation costs would be withheld from their pay, a condition that had not been contractually stated. Food was mouldy, facilities lacked running water, and housing consisted of containers shared with 20 people. The workers were initially underpaid, and after a while the hours of work were reduced. With reduced pay and hours, the workers could not pay the interest on their debts. The threat of being sent back if they ceased to work meant the workers were trapped. Global Horizons 'recruited' around 1100 Thai nationals between 2003 and 2006.[49] In 2016, a district judge in the US ordered the company to pay US$7 658 500 in damages to claimants.[50] Yet, there has not been reform of the temporary worker programs in the US, so they remain rife with abuse.[51] The Department of Agriculture estimates that in recent years around half of hired farmworkers were undocumented.[52]

Other instances of modern slavery in the agricultural industry are indirectly caused by innovative business practices. For example, bananas are an important export commodity in the Philippines. Land reform initiatives in this country saw plots of land being allocated to farmers by the state. The government promoted Agribusiness Venture Agreements, which allowed the private sector to provide farmers with support services and access to capital. However, as part of long-term contractual agreements with large multinational agricultural companies, Filipino banana farmers often became indebted by paying in advance for land preparation, maintenance and harvesting.

Many contracts specify that farmers are required to buy all production materials from the company, with farmers having no say about the type and cost of inputs. Produce is sold at a fixed price, rather than according to the market value. The contract prohibits farmers from growing others' crops on their land.[53] Such exploitative arrangements mean that many farming families are pushed into debt for generations,[54] which means they cannot pursue other employment options and opportunities.

Poverty and income inequality are key antecedents of modern slavery. In agricultural supply chains, only a small portion of the price that consumers pay for produce is shared with farmers. In Ecuador, the world's largest exporter of bananas, small-scale producers are left with 3 per cent of the end consumer price, half of what it was in 1992, while international supermarkets sourcing from the Ecuadorian banana supply chain have seen their share of the consumer price increase to 40 per cent.[55] Consumer prices for oranges and orange juice have increased 50 per cent globally since the 1990s. In Brazil, which produces one-third of the world's oranges and 40 per cent of orange juice, the share going to small-scale farmers has shrunk from 17 per cent to 4 per cent in this period, while supermarkets and brands have increased their share.[56]

Aggregated globally across all agricultural goods, in 2011 farmers shared in 14 per cent of the end consumer price, down from 16 per cent in 1995. The share of the end consumer price increased for owners and investors (5 per cent) and high-skilled labourers (3 per cent) in food supply chains, while it declined for those providing medium- (1 per cent) and low-skilled labour (7 per cent).[57] This decline of labour income breeds poverty. Meanwhile cost pressures undermine working conditions by increasing flexible employment, excessive overtime and wage cuts.[58] In the worst cases, plantations and farms resort to the increased use of child labour (which already affects 98 million children[59]) and forced labour (already affecting 1.1 million people[60]). Global supply chains, therefore, not only link us all to modern slavery, as a production regime they frequently generate the preconditions necessary for modern slavery to flourish.

Civil society makes continuous efforts to raise awareness of modern slavery in the production of everyday goods. In 2018, a large vending machine was placed in central London. Inside sat an actor, portraying a slave, dispensing lemons, tomatoes, sugar, avocado and eggs at the touch of a button. The campaign, initiated by the Wilberforce Institute at Hull University, was meant to raise awareness of the estimated 136 000 people trapped in slavery in Britain, and draw attention to the manner in which people's lives as consumers are made possible by modern slavery. In a report published by the Wilberforce Institute, one-third of British people surveyed were not aware that slaves were used to produce fresh foods. One in five did not believe that slavery occurs in Britain, and one in ten said that while slavery existed in the past, it no longer happens today.[61]

Those consumers who are aware of modern slavery are routinely misinformed: 'The stories that companies are telling us about efforts to fight forced labour in supply chains are … basically fairy tales'.[62] A 2018 study involving interviews and surveys with tea and cocoa workers from 22 tea plantations in India and 74 cocoa communities in Ghana found that ethical certification schemes are failing to create environments that are free from exploitation and forced labour.[63] The report found little difference in conditions on certified and non-certified sites: all surveyed workers lived below the poverty line, while workers on certified farms were often treated worse, facing beatings, sexual violence and having wages withheld.[64] Consumers are too often left ignorant of the conditions in which goods are produced.

Modern slavery and luxury goods

To a large degree, modern slavery is able persist due to the ignorance and indifference of governments, companies and consumers. Governments do not want to stifle economic growth, jeopardise their export position, create 'unnecessary red tape' for companies or – if they are corrupt – stop profiting from bribes and kickbacks. Governments in developing regions and in affluent countries are beholden to the neoliberal policy agenda, best described by the motto 'Let business be business'. At best this policy approach results in an arm's-length attitude to companies and markets, and in the worst-case scenarios it results in a hands-off attitude where companies and industries are left to regulate themselves. Companies, both large and small, generally do not want to endanger their financial bottom lines and shareholder returns, and not all are keen on the prospect of complying with 'cumbersome' legislation and social standards.

Similarly, many consumers do not want to pay more for everyday commodities such as food or for luxury goods such as electric cars and the latest mobile phones. Yet, problematically, if you have a mobile phone, tablet, laptop or computer, you are connected to modern slavery. Few people are aware of the mineral cobalt and the conditions in which it is obtained. Demand for this mineral has surged with the increased production of lithium-ion batteries, in which cobalt is used, and is predicted to swell from 53 000 tonnes in 2015 to more than 120 000 tonnes by 2025.[65] With demand for this resource increasing, the pressure on suppliers will not end any time soon. Around two-thirds of the world's cobalt is sourced from the Democratic Republic of Congo.[66] The majority comes from industrial mines, while about one-fifth is mined informally, according to Amnesty International.[67] The Democratic Republic of Congo is home to several forms of modern slavery, including forced labour enforced by armed groups, debt bondage, sexual slavery, forced marriage, the use of children by armed groups, and other forms of child slavery.[68]

Thousands of impoverished people have made their way to the Democratic Republic of Congo in search of cobalt and better fortunes. Footage obtained by the *Washington Post* shows people descending into small hand-dug holes, in conditions that defy even basic safety standards. Men, women and children dig in these artisanal mines, in which there have been numerous death and injuries. Tellingly, those that search for cobalt do not see themselves as miners. Rather, they call themselves *creuseurs* or 'diggers'.[69] It is estimated there are around 110 000 to 150 000 of these artisanal miners – which includes children as young as seven.[70] UNICEF estimates that around 40 000 children worked in mines across the Democratic Republic of Congo in 2014; Amnesty International considers this figure to be a severe underestimate, considering the recent increase in the global demand for cobalt.[71]

The work performed by children in these artisanal

mines falls under the worst forms of child labour, as defined by the ILO. This means that it concerns work 'which, by its nature or the circumstances in which it is carried out, is likely to harm the health, safety or morals of children'.[72] Children experience physical abuse, drug abuse, sexual exploitation and violence, often at the hands of security guards who patrol mine sites. Children are often forced to pay concessions to the guards to enter mines, and frequently have their mineral yields taken from them. While the children work mostly independently, they sell their yields to traders: 'I sold to *négociants* who have scales. But some of the others did not have scales and just estimated the weight and were not fair. They exploited the children, they paid us less than they paid the adults'.[73] Some children had to work for certain traders to pay off debts, after having borrowed money from them: 'Sometimes if we didn't get a product we would go to a *négociant* and borrow money and then had to work for him for the next day'.[74]

Research by Amnesty International revealed that electronics and car companies are not making enough effort to tackle child and forced labour in cobalt supply chains. In 2016, it concluded that all of the 26 companies it had assessed failed to conduct human rights due diligence in line with international standards.[75] A year later, it concluded that half of the 28 companies it had assessed failed to demonstrate even minimal compliance with due diligence standards.[76] There are some initiatives within the industry. In addition to efforts by individual companies, electronics and car manufacturers have created the Responsible Business Alliance, an industry initiative to improve conditions in supply chains.[77] Its board is entirely made up of company executives; companies join by adopting the code of conduct, and are 'held accountable' through self-assessment. Funding is derived from the member companies in the sectors it monitors. For such reasons, industry-led initiatives are often considered to be less progressive compared to initiatives that involve multiple stakeholders.[78]

More reputable is the Extractive Industries Transparency Initiative, which consists of states, companies, civil society and institutional investors. Membership is voluntary, and members must comply with its transparency principles. Nonetheless, 50 studies assessed its achievements and found mixed results.[79] Institutionally, it has become a well-known brand, yet membership is thin in many regions. It has been less successful in realising operational goals: the scope of requirements is criticised and there is little evidence of capacity building and increased public debate. There is also limited evidence of reducing corruption, increasing aid or improving working and living standards. Transparency initiatives are said only to be effective if resource-rich countries have a strong civil society, where media can freely publicise, and stakeholders are able and willing to hold governments and companies to account.[80]

With the surge in electric vehicles being sold globally, the demand for cobalt is likely to grow.

Although technology to create lithium-ion batteries without cobalt is currently being developed, lowering the demand for cobalt will only apply a temporary patch to a broken system of cross-border sourcing and production. Cobalt is but one raw material that is in high demand in global supply chains; the mineral mica is another, as discussed. High demand in global supply chains for any commodity sourced from any impoverished region will result in the same kinds of human rights violations.

Sourcing exclusively from regulated mines does not offer a watertight solution either. Artisanally mined cobalt can enter the supply chain at any stage[81], in a similar way as illegally mined tin from Indonesia entered Apple's supply chain.[82] Arguably, cobalt does not have to be sourced from conflict regions alone. It can also be sourced from countries with stricter regulation and enforcement, such as Australia. However, removing or lowering demand for a commodity that is tainted by modern slavery or sourcing materials from a different region neither provides a structural solution to supply chain exploitation, nor does it help locals to share in a country's wealth of natural resources.[83] Unless public institutions enforce more effective governance and stop relying on self-regulation by companies and industry bodies, civil society organisations have no choice but to adopt a responsive stance and expose modern slavery wherever it rears its ugly head.

Governments can be complicit

Apart from the indifference and negligence of governments, there are also governments that actively promote and benefit from slave labour. While modern slavery can be connected to companies and consumers through supply chains, it can also be linked to governments. Several governments around the world use prison labour or conscripted labour, or force their citizens to work in government-owned industries. Furthermore, a fact that is often overlooked is that governments are commonly the largest procurers of goods and services in a country, which means that they too can be connected to modern slavery through their sourcing decisions.

State-sanctioned forced labour occurs on a large scale in North Korea. It is estimated that one in ten people living in North Korea, 2.6 million people, are subjected to forced labour and exploitation by the state in sectors such as agriculture and construction.[84] They produce an estimated US$975 million worth of value each year.[85] The Australian-based Walk Free Foundation interviewed 50 North Korean defectors who escaped the country between 2011 and 2016. All of them described work organised by the state, and indicated they had either not been paid or wages were subject to significant state-held deductions.[86] People of the lowest class of forced labourers, called *dolgyeokdae*, are required to demonstrate their devotion to the supreme leader by performing heavy labour for years on end.

North Korean authorities proudly show these workers on national television to demonstrate their 'loyalty'.[87] Workers who do not obey orders are imprisoned in work camps.[88] It may seem that slave labour in North Korea would not play a role in the global economy, due to economic sanctions and its isolated status, or that it is not connected to companies and consumers through global supply chains. This is not true.

For example, China imports US$1 billion worth of coal each year from North Korea, which is dug out by miners who toil because they have to, rather than out of choice.[89] After coal and other minerals, textiles are North Korea's second biggest export. In 2016, North Korea exported US$752 million worth of textiles. Chinese textile companies increasingly use North Korean factories to take advantage of cheap labour, while labelling these as 'Made in China' and exporting them around the world. Workers are paid a fraction of Chinese wages: from a minimum monthly amount of US$75 to an average of US$160, compared to wages of US$450 to US$750 a month in China.[90]

North Korean garment factories are state-owned and in high demand. 'We've been trying to get some of our clothes made in North Korea, but the factories are fully booked at the moment', said a Korean-Chinese businesswoman. A Korean-Chinese businessman added: 'North Korean workers can produce 30 per cent more clothes each day than a Chinese worker … factory workers can't just go to the toilet whenever they feel like, otherwise they think it slows down the whole assembly line'.[91] In 2016, it was revealed that the Australian surf brand giant Rip Curl sold clothing made in North Korea that was worth millions of dollars. The company blamed one of its subcontractors.[92]

Apart from outsourcing production to North Korea, Chinese companies also employ thousands of North Korean workers in China. They earn about US$300 a month, half of what the average Chinese workers earns. They get to keep around one-third of their earnings; the rest goes to their North Korean government handlers. According to a Korean-Chinese businesswoman, North Korean workers 'aren't like Chinese factory workers who just work for the money. North Koreans have a different attitude – they believe they are working for their country, for their leader'.[93] Around 200 000 North Koreans work outside their country as part of a state-sponsored system of exported forced labour.

In 2018, an undercover investigation discovered North Korean workers labouring in China, Russia and Poland.[94] In Russia, North Koreans were found working in construction. These workers have to hand over most of their earnings to their 'captain'. In Polish shipyards, it is thought about 800 North Koreans work as welders and labourers; most of them live at the shipyard in makeshift accommodation. In 2017, the UN announced new sanctions that would put an end to North Koreans working abroad, giving companies two years to comply.[95] Yet a lot more needs to be done to ensure that companies and consumers are not connected to North Korean slave labour, especially in light of the summit between Kim Jong-un and Donald Trump, and discussions about lifting economic sanctions and 'opening up' the country.[96]

State-sanctioned slave labour can play a substantial role in commodity production in the formal economy, and can potentially affect any company and consumer in the world through cross-border sourcing and production. State-sanctioned slave labour is particularly common in the cotton sector. In Uzbekistan and Turkmenistan each year during the harvest season, citizens are forced out of their regular jobs to spend weeks picking cotton.[97] People are given a daily quota; failure to meet this target could mean they lose their job or face harassment. Farmers have to grow cotton or face financial penalties or removal from the land they farm. Businesses are forced to contribute financially if they want to stay open during the harvest.[98] In recent years, many companies and countries have announced they would stop sourcing cotton from these countries. In 2018, the US imposed a ban on cotton products from Turkmenistan, yet it continues to import cotton and related goods from Uzbekistan.[99]

According to the ILO, Uzbekistan has made significant progress towards banning state-sanctioned forced labour in the cotton sector. Based on 11 000 interviews with people involved in the harvest, the agency said that of about 2.6 million people who temporarily pick cotton every year, in 2018, 93 per cent did so voluntarily. Several human rights groups have disputed this claim. The Uzbek-German Forum for Human Rights monitored the 2018 harvest in seven regions and interviewed more than 300 people; it was found they were forced to work or pay for workers to take their place.[100] Human Rights Watch also disputes the claims, stating that even 'if 93 percent of cotton pickers are working voluntarily, that would still leave about 180,000 who are not'.[101] It found several issues with the methods used by the ILO: it allowed the involvement of government and government-aligned organisations, which means that the monitoring was not independent, while many interviewees appeared to have been briefed in advance.[102] Disturbingly, the World Bank is funding agricultural projects in Uzbekistan worth half a billion US dollars, and therefore appears to be funding and profiting from forced labour.[103]

Another example of state-sanctioned forced labour is goods produced through prison labour. Some companies consciously use prison labour to reduce wage costs; other companies unknowingly do so through negligence or ignorance. The notion of forced prison labour came to the attention of the general public after several notes – written by exploited labourers – were found in items sold in the US. In 2017, a woman in Arizona bought a purse at Walmart and found a note describing forced labour conditions in China: 'Prisoners in the Yingshan Prison in Guangxi, China are working 14 hours every day with no break/rest at noon, continue working overtime until 12 midnight', the note read, 'whoever does not finish his work will be beaten'.[104] The letter was signed by a man serving a 15-year prison sentence. Walmart cut ties with the supplier who had been subcontracting to Yingshan Prison. Similarly, in 2012, a Kmart shopper found a note describing working conditions in a detention facility in China; in 2014, a woman found a disturbing note in a bag purchased from a luxury New York department store, written by a man who was forced to work long hours in a Chinese prison factory. The worker was tracked down and later released.[105] China has around 2.3 million prisoners and those who are able to work must do so to achieve 'reform through labour'.[106]

Chinese prison labour is also used in the manufacturing of electronics. A few years ago, the airlines Qantas, British Airways and Emirates were linked to Chinese prison labour: the disposable headsets aboard the aeroplanes of these carriers were allegedly made by Chinese inmates who received physical punishment if they missed their production targets.[107] More recently, an investigation by the *Financial Times* found Chinese prisoners assembling wiring that goes into household appliances: 'We did nothing but work', says an ex-prisoner, who was ordered to bundle wires together for a medium electronics company that supplied to the South Korean multinational LG, who has since severed the relationship.

Garlic is another commodity produced in China that is heavily tainted by prison labour. Former prisoners of a facility in Jinxiang – a county that produces 80 per cent of the world's garlic exports – say the acids in the garlic melts fingernails, and that detainees who cannot use their hands bite off the garlic skins with their teeth. Posing as a garlic importer, the *Financial Times* spoke to a company that uses prison labour: 'our area exports peeled garlic to many countries ... foreign demand from developed countries for peeled garlic is growing bigger and bigger'. When contacted later by the newspaper for an official comment, the exporter stated it did not ship garlic overseas and sold only domestically. The US sources 80 per cent of all its fresh garlic from China.[108]

Exporting prison-produced goods is illegal under domestic and international trade laws. Customs and Border Protection in the US can issue a 'withhold release order' if a complaint is raised against a foreign producer, and if it is suspected that imported foods are tainted by forced labour, shipments are held at the border. At the time of writing, of the 46 withhold release orders, 32 were against Chinese producers.[109] There is, nevertheless, copious evidence of prison labour used in the production of internationally exported goods, and there is reason to look at the US as well. Its prison population is similar in size to China's, but it has the highest incarceration rate in the world: of every 100 000 people, 655 are in prison.[110] If its prison population were a city, it would be the country's fifth largest.

US prison labour is a billion-dollar industry.[111] Thirty-seven states allow the use of prison labour by private companies.[112] In eight states, prisoners are not paid for their work in state-run facilities. The country-wide average for inmates receiving the least for their work is 14 cents per hour; the average for those earning the most is 63 cents per hour.[113] In 2018, detainees went on strike over working conditions and racist sentencing policies.[114] While prison labour in the US occurs on a 'voluntary' basis, there have been reports of penalties such as solitary confinement and reduced food portions if inmates refuse to work.[115] The reduction in food means that detainees have no other choice but to work or purchase extra food at inflated prices.[116]

Apart from the various forms of state-sanctioned forced labour, the state can also be connected to labour exploitation through public spending. For example, prisoners in English jails were found to be providing a range of services to public institutions for as little as £4 a week. One of the most lucrative contracts involved the National Health Service using prison labour to do laundry for hospitals.[117] On average, in the 36 countries that are part of the OECD, public procurement constitutes 12 per cent of the annual gross domestic product. Public health spending, on average, represents the largest share of expenditure, accounting for almost one-third of public procurement in OECD countries.[118] The sizeable volume of (health) spending and the complex contracting links to the private sector exposes governments to various labour and human rights risks.

As governments around the world increasingly outsource public services and pursue savings to balance their budgets, cost pressures are generated that can affect workers further up the supply chain. There are many examples of medical commodities that are tainted by labour and human rights abuses.[119] There are 150 billion pairs of medical rubber gloves produced annually. Investigations found that migrant workers at a Malaysian production site of Ansell (an Australian glove company) had to pay labour hire companies' fees equal to three months' wages, and had their passports confiscated while employed. At Malaysian company Top Glove, the world's largest glove manufacturer, there have been reports of illegal detention of employees and beatings by security guards.[120]

A 2018 investigation found that migrant workers had to pay fees to recruitment agents, sometimes funded by high-interest loans, resulting in debt bondage.[121] The production of scissors, forceps, scalpels and sutures is also linked to exploitation: the city of Sialkot in Pakistan produces 80 per cent of the world's surgical instruments, which are, in part, produced in sweatshops that use child labour.[122] Manufacturers of theatre and patient gowns have also been criticised. At factories in India and Pakistan that produce patient clothing, workwear, sheets, towels and other textiles, excessive and illegal overtime is demanded of workers, while refusal to work overtime or attempts to create a union result in dismissal.[123]

Raw materials used in the production of these goods, such as rubber, iron and cotton, have been linked to child and forced labour.[124]

Unfortunately, the reality is that too many governments, companies and consumers have become trapped in a pattern of minimal reform and frequent denial. This state of affairs has prevented structural change from occurring, allowing labour and human rights abuses to continue. Theoretically, civil society organisations and consumers are a powerful combination in effecting change, yet in practice the consciousness-raising moments that they manage to generate are too easily neutralised. Companies have little difficulty in reaffirming their legitimacy with investors and consumers, thereby neutralising any potential reputational damage. Despite a range of companies being implicated in labour and human rights abuses, companies have an easy time convincing governments that the neoliberal regime of self-regulation and corporate social responsibility is functioning.

There is another problem with relying on civil society to hold companies and governments to account for using modern slavery. In many countries in which modern slavery is prevalent, civil society is often hindered in its effective functioning or is actively oppressed by authorities. In cases where local labour and human rights organisations cannot perform their work unimpeded, it often falls to international organisations to step into the breach. Yet these organisations may be hampered by lack of an 'on the ground' presence and are easily labelled and potentially de-legitimised as a 'foreign influence'. In the absence of meaningful reforms by national and international public institutions, this impasse allows modern slavery to persist, if not flourish. Progress in the fight against modern slavery can only be achieved if this cycle is broken.

3

Emergence of the corporate social conscience?

Companies always talk about being on a human rights 'journey'. It is a long and winding journey with many stops along the way. They are never on a journey to profit. They make profit happen quickly. A human rights journey, however, is generally less critical. But it's hard to think of a journey that is more pressing than one that ends in freeing people from slavery. The fact is that companies have tremendous influence over our daily lives and often have the leverage and power to determine whether that impact is positive or negative. If you can change corporate behaviour, you can change people's lives in an immediate and tangible way.

The interconnections between business operations

and concerns for human rights are not new, rather they have steadily risen in profile in recent years. Before 2015, when the UK established a *Modern Slavery Act*, few people would have been familiar with the term 'modern slavery'. Now anyone can go online and calculate their slavery footprint and assess if the coffee they drink, the fish they eat, the shoes they wear and the phone they use are likely to be the products of slave labour. Different companies have different motivations for why they should, or do, care about human rights; for many, the 'journey' begins with an attempt to salvage their reputation and (sometimes) ends with more substantive efforts to understand and address the myriad ways that companies can and do negatively impact human rights. What began in earnest in the 1970s as a movement couched in the somewhat vague and amorphous language of 'corporate social responsibility' has morphed into more solid references to labour rights and human rights and an acknowledgment that business does indeed have a responsibility to respect human rights. Some companies get this message quicker than others and are acting to integrate human rights into their business operations. Other companies are still twiddling their thumbs.

The current focus on modern slavery makes some human rights activists wary about whether such a narrow focus means that more 'run-of-the-mill' labour rights violations are in danger of being overlooked. The death of more than 1100 workers in Bangladesh in 2013 was directly attributable to a failure in basic checks on building safety and overdevelopment that lacked government oversight. But behind the disaster was a history of worker suppression in Bangladesh's garment factories where workers were enduring long hours for low pay, filling orders for major American, European and other international brands, and who lacked the voice and support to refuse to re-enter the building on that fateful day on 24 April 2013. The modern slavery debate is one part of a much bigger picture that should and must include a focus on the role business should play in supporting worker empowerment and unionisation and in preventing discrimination, harassment and health and safety violations. Companies that discover cases of modern slavery in their supply chain will quickly realise such gross violations of human rights do not occur in isolation. Workers who are subjected to forced labour or human trafficking are also likely to experience discrimination, harassment and wage theft. The origins of the current modern slavery debates stem from a push to increase corporate awareness of human rights and engender responsibility to act to prevent workplace abuses. However, as the ensuing discussion makes apparent, developing a corporate social conscience is not the same as implementing operational changes that acknowledge basic respect for workers' rights.

The early days of corporate social responsibility

In the mid-1970s, activists focused their ire on the Swiss-based company Nestlé's marketing tactics that promoted the use of infant formula over breastfeeding. Activists argued that the company was targeting mothers in the developing world and getting them hooked on baby formula to the detriment of babies' health. Nestlé was labelled as a 'baby killer' and went to court to try and save its reputation.[1] Social rights groups launched a highly visible campaign against the company and encouraged a boycott of its products. Nestlé responded with a libel suit. In 1978, the US Senate held a public hearing into the promotion of breastmilk substitutes in developing countries. Under questioning from US Senator Edward Kennedy about Nestlé's responsibility for the use of breast milk substitutes in areas of poverty, the then President of Nestlé Brazil, Oswaldo Ballarin, responded that the company should not have that responsibility and the boycott against Nestlé was an indirect attack on the free world economic system.[2] The Senate hearing concluded that there was indeed a global problem and called for a universal marketing code to safeguard infant health. In 1979, the World Health Organization and UNICEF joined the call for the development of an international code of marketing and global action intensified. In 1981, the International Code of Marketing of Breast-milk Substitutes was released by the World Health Organization and a few years later, after facing sustained public pressure, Nestlé agreed to abide by the code.

However, Nestlé is a much bigger company than one that just sells infant formula. It is one of the world's largest food and beverage companies with more than 2000 brands in its stable. These days it boasts revenue of US$91 billion and its brands include Nescafé, Kit Kat, Uncle Tobys and Purina to name but a few.[3] But more brands means more diversified global supply chains, more workers spread all over the world and greater potential for human rights problems.

In 2005, 30 years after it had stared down activists over its marketing campaign for infant formula, Nestlé was sued in the US for its alleged use of child and slave labour in the Côte d'Ivoire in its chocolate supply chain.[4] The lawsuit alleged that workers in Nestlé's supply chain were forced to work long hours without pay, kept under lock and key when not working, and suffered physical abuse by those guarding them. Nestlé itself was not directly employing any of these workers, but these workers are crucial cogs in the wheels of Nestlé's long and complex supply chain and when enough mud is thrown, it sticks. These same workers also produce goods for many other large companies, but the lawsuits were brought against Nestlé, in part because of its global visibility. Precisely because it is such large and powerful company that sits at the top of the supply chain, it is argued that the company should accept some responsibility for the way in which the workers at the bottom of that chain are treated, even if they are not the company's direct employees. If Nestlé cares about the quality of its products, shouldn't it also care about the quality with which workers in its supply chain are treated, the ones who make the chocolate and coffee we consume?

Nestlé's story is one that could be written about many companies. Human rights are only a recent agenda item in many boardroom discussions, and they are still yet to be seriously considered by many companies. Nestlé's response to the allegations about its marketing practices in the 1970s and 1980s was slow and often misdirected. Its early reaction to jump in and sue activists for libel meant that while it might score an early victory in a court of law, it was likely to lose in the court of public opinion. But in 2014, when new allegations surfaced against Nestlé that tied brutal and largely unregulated working conditions at sea in harvesting seafood for their Purina brand pet foods, the company opened its doors wide and launched an investigation into the allegations in collaboration with an independent non-profit organisation, Verité. A year-long investigation uncovered some atrocious working conditions in some of Nestlé's seafood supply chains and in 2015 the company made the report public.[5]

The problems were not isolated to Nestlé's products, and the investigation found that virtually all US and European companies that were buying seafood from Thailand were exposed to the same risks of abuse in their supply chains. But Nestlé owned this problem, made it transparent and took the initiative to combat it. That doesn't mean it has solved it, but it was a markedly different approach from where the company started on its journey four decades earlier. Nestlé now talks about creating 'shared value', that is, creating value for shareholders and society by having 'a positive impact on society while we grow our business'.[6] In 2019, Nestlé made public a list of its cocoa suppliers in Côte d'Ivoire and Ghana along with its suppliers for a number of other priority commodities, including palm oil, soya, paper and meat. So, what has changed in the last 40 years and why do (some) companies now more obviously care (or at least profess to care) about human rights? And why should companies care?

Corporate social responsibility or a sideshow?

The role that corporations play in domestic and international economies is fundamental. Their effect on human rights is equally important as they have the potential to make a direct and enduring impact on people's lives. Business can be a transformative force for good. Through commercial activity driven by corporations, jobs and wages are made available, goods and services are provided, and taxes are paid, enabling governments to provide further services. In 2018, Walmart continued its reign at the top of the Fortune 500 with revenues in excess of US$500 billion.[7] Walmart employs more than 2.2 million people globally and is the world's third largest employer, behind only the militaries of the US and China. There is no doubt that a globalised economy has generated millions of jobs over the last quarter century. It has lifted hundreds of millions of people out of extreme poverty,[8] but not every job is a 'good' job. Walmart, while credited with providing jobs to thousands, also has a litany of worker exploitation complaints against it.[9]

Some business practices erode respect for, or simply disregard, human rights. Companies, both local and global, have been and continue to be minor and major abusers of human rights. Some companies are guilty of treating workers badly, in terms of pay, conditions and workplace safety; some pollute the environment in ways that have dramatic and serious effects far beyond their immediate surroundings; some discriminate against Indigenous peoples, certain ethnic or religious groups, women or people with disabilities, and on grounds of sexuality; and some work alongside (or inside) governments that perpetrate gross human rights abuses.[10] Others use modern-day slaves in their supply chains.

When the concept of corporate social responsibility (CSR) started to gain prominence in the 1970s, many in the business world dismissed the concept as one not only superfluous to business but potentially harmful to companies. CSR roughly translates as an idea that

PRECARIOUS LABOUR

A study of Walmart's supply chain in Bangladesh, Cambodia, India and Indonesia from 2012 to 2016 highlighted the precarious nature of work it provides.[11] Reports garnered via focus-group discussions and interviews, including 344 workers from 80 Walmart supplier factories, identified persistent rights violations. In Cambodia, forced overtime was found to be a characteristic management practice in all 14 Walmart supplier factories. Workers reported that the standard work day was 10 to 14 hours per day – well beyond the set eight-hour work day established under Cambodian law – and workers reported they could not leave the factory before overtime hours were completed and that sick leave was usually refused. Since the vast majority of workers were employed on short, fixed-duration contracts, they were vulnerable to termination if they resisted these practices. Illegal use of short-term contracts is common in the Bangladeshi, Cambodian, Indian and Indonesian garment industries – including in Walmart's supply chains. Threats of non-renewal of contracts undermine workers' ability to demand safe workplaces, to exercise their rights to freedom of association and to refuse overtime work.

business should voluntarily operate in a manner that delivers economic, social and environmental benefits for all stakeholders including its workers, customers and shareholders. In 1970, when economist Milton Friedman declared that 'there is one and only one social responsibility of business – to use its resources and engage in activities designed to increase its profits'[12] there were probably few in the business world who disagreed with him. But with the burgeoning growth of global corporations over the past few decades and the increasing inequality between what is earned in the boardroom versus on the factory floor,[13] there have been parallel concerns to find ways of regulating the deleterious impacts on human rights by the ever-increasing number of companies whose corporate tentacles stretch around the globe.

While Friedman largely dismissed the somewhat amorphous concept of companies having any social responsibilities, he did acknowledge that a company could not pursue profits at all costs. He wrote:

> In a free enterprise, private property system, a corporate executive is an employee of the owners of the business. He has direct responsibility to his employers. That responsibility is to conduct the business in accordance with their desires, which generally will be to make as much money as possible while conforming to the basic rules of

> the society, both those embodied in law and those embodied in ethical custom.[14]

While Friedman relied on a narrow definition of a corporation's potential social responsibility, he did recognise each company's responsibility to conform to the basic rules of society, including those based on ethics. Times have changed since 1970 and there is an increased expectation that companies will stand up and champion social causes, including those related to human rights. A 2017 survey of 1000 US consumers found that 66 per cent believe it's important for brands to take public stands on social and political issues and that brands are most credible when an issue directly affects their customers (47 per cent), employees (40 per cent) and business operations (31 per cent).[15] The 2019 Edelman Trust Barometer supports this by noting that 67 per cent of employees surveyed expected that employers would join them in taking action on societal issues.[16]

The campaign against the use of modern slavery in supply chains ticks all these boxes in terms of relevance to customers, consumers and corporate supply chains, but the personal connection is not always made between the clothes we wear and the actions that might be taken to ensure that they are made and sourced in a socially responsible way. These consumer survey results echo findings by Deloitte in 2016: that 56 per cent of millennials will exclude from their shopping lists the companies that are not operating sustainably, while 49 per cent

GARMENT WORKERS

Radhika, a garment worker in a H&M supply chain factory in Bangalore, India, described the afternoon when her batch supervisor threw her on the floor, kicked her and hit her repeatedly on her breasts. This incident took place in late 2017 and she was abused simply because she failed to meet her production quota. She returned to work despite the harassment as it was the only means to escape extreme poverty: 'My husband passed away and I have a physically challenged daughter who cannot work. That is why I need the job. I suffer a lot to earn my livelihood'.[17]

Garment workers are predominantly female. For example, 90–95 per cent of Cambodian garment workers are women,[18] while in Bangladesh, women comprise almost 80 per cent of the workforce.[19] The patterns of abuse against female workers are often gendered, as the value of their labour is considered lower than that of male workers, and unequal power relations between male supervisors and female workers lend to greater instances of physical and verbal abuse and sexual violence.[20]

will refuse to work for companies that go against their personal ethics.[21] However, these principled views don't always translate into concrete actions that filter down to improved conditions for workers on the factory floor.

While increased consumer focus on social responsibility can only be a good thing for the global corporate sustainability agenda, it is not clear that all companies have received and understood this message (or that consumers will necessarily put their money where their mouth is[22]). However, through both legal and non-legal developments in recent decades, we have witnessed the emergence of a broader understanding of the social responsibilities of a company that seeks to embed respect for human rights in mainstream business operations, rather than simply treating a concern for rights as an optional extra.

Business and human rights

Significant developments have been taking place in factories, fields and workplaces all over the world where people have been pushing and prodding corporations to adopt operational changes to achieve sustained compliance with human rights. Sometimes businesses have been proactive in seeking such changes, at other times they have been reluctant or simply absent.

Activism against corporate irresponsibility in the 1970s, 1980s and 1990s aimed at companies such as Shell, Nike, Exxon, Disney and many others forced (some) companies to try and tackle their impact on human rights. Most of these efforts have been voluntary, rather than required by law, and depend in part on the co-option of corporate leaders. Some are efforts by single companies, others are collaborative initiatives between non-governmental organisations (NGOs), unions, companies and/or governments, and some are high-level initiatives instigated by the United Nations (UN), the International Labour Organization (ILO) or the Organisation for Economic Co-operation and Development (OECD).

In 2000, the UN established the Global Compact as an attempt to harness the power of the private sector to improve basic respect for workers and the communities in which they operate. The Global Compact calls on companies to voluntarily 'embrace and enact' a set of ten principles relating to human rights, labour rights, the environment, and anti-corruption. By participating, companies agree to incorporate the principles in their day-to-day operations and issue an annual public progress report. The Global Compact is a tool to educate companies about human rights, and counts more than 13 530 organisations (businesses, governments, NGOs, universities and other entities)[23] as participants. It is a useful tool for educating companies about human rights but it is not a forum for getting them to actually comply with human rights standards.

The establishment in 2011 of the Guiding Principles on Business and Human Rights[24] (UN Guiding

Principles) by the UN Human Rights Council was a major stepping stone in affirming that companies should not focus on the generation of profits without also considering their broader impact. The UN Guiding Principles are designed to provide general guidance and direction on how business and governments should better incorporate human rights into their operations. The principles acknowledge that while governments should protect human rights, companies also have a responsibility to respect human rights and in so doing, affirmed the centrality of human rights concerns to business. For many (but not all) companies, the question is no longer: 'Do we have an obligation to address human rights?' Rather, it is: 'How do we do it, at what cost, and with whom do we collaborate in addressing the problems that exist?'

The OECD and the ILO have also developed high-level guidance documents that encourage companies to abide by international labour and human rights standards that are primarily dependent on governments encouraging companies to do so.[25] For example, the OECD Guidelines for Multinational Enterprises is a set of recommendations targeted at companies that come under the jurisdiction of OECD member governments (for example, a company headquartered in Australia but operating a mine in the Philippines should abide by these guidelines because Australia is an OECD member even if the Philippines is not). First launched in 1976 with only a passing reference to human rights, they were updated in 2011 to incorporate the tenets of the UN Guiding Principles. The OECD Guidelines are voluntary in their application and multinational companies are invited to incorporate the OECD Guidelines into their operations. The OECD Guidelines include a complaint procedure that allows civil society and others to submit complaints concerning alleged breaches of the OECD Guidelines to a government's national contact point.[26]

In 2015, the UN launched the Sustainable Development Goals (SDGs), which are an evolution of the Millennium Development Goals crafted in 2000 and which acknowledge the fundamental role companies can play in reducing poverty and inequality and spurring economic growth. The SDGs have turned into a global industry. Today, there are countless conferences based on SDG themes. Billions of dollars of investment have been spent and numerous working groups, task forces, family foundations, philanthropic endeavours and government delegations have formed part of a growing army dedicated to spreading the SDG gospel. All of this is fantastic, but it is not always easy to separate the SDG industry from its impact and what changes are implemented at ground level. Out of thousands of words of text in the SDGs, 'human rights' is mentioned only once, but SDG 8.7 specifically sets the global task of eradicating forced labour, ending modern slavery and human trafficking by 2030. While the SDGs were primarily negotiated by governments, they acknowledge

MANUS ISLAND

A company, G4S, was contracted by the Australian Government to oversee management and security at the Manus Island centre (in Papua New Guinea) between February 2013 and March 2014. The centre was an offshore facility set up by the Australian Government to hold refugees and asylum seekers in immigration detention. Over this period, the detention centre was repeatedly criticised by human rights organisations including the UN High Commissioner for Refugees for breaching basic minimum standards of care. In February 2014, one detainee was killed, and more than 60 others were injured in an outbreak of violence.[27]

In 2014, a complaint was filed under the OECD Guidelines for Multinational Enterprises, in Australia and the UK (where G4S head office is located), by UK NGO Rights and Accountability and the Australian-based NGO Human Rights Law Centre. The complaint alleged breaches of the Guidelines relating to G4S's complicity in an unlawful detention regime, its failure to maintain basic human rights standards at the detention centre, and its failure to protect detainees from violence, including assaults by its own employees. The Australian national contact point for the OECD rejected the complaint at the initial assessment stage, partly on the basis it was not the role of the Australian office to issue commentary on government policies or law. The OECD Guidelines offered no recourse to resolving this problem. The UK also rejected the complaint.

In December 2016, a class-action lawsuit was filed on behalf of 1900 detainees at the Manus Island centre who suffered injury as a result of alleged conduct by the Australian Government, G4S and Transfield (later Broadspectrum). Many of the issues raised in the OECD complaint were referenced in the claim. In April 2016, the detention centre was ruled illegal and unconstitutional by the Papua New Guinea Supreme Court, and in 2017 the Australian Government agreed to settle the lawsuit and pay more than AU$70 million in compensation to the detainees.

The Refugee Council of Australia notes that as of March 2019, it is estimated that there are still more than 500 people detained on Manus Island.

that collaboration between the private sector and the public is required to achieve their goals. In essence, the SDGs emphasise that everyone has a role to play in eradicating modern slavery. But sometimes the danger of relying on the notion of shared responsibility is that when everyone is responsible, no-one is.

All of these initiatives, each in its own way, aim to elevate human rights as both a corporate concern and a responsibility. Each of them offers guidance on the centrality of human rights to business, but none of them legally mandate what companies can and cannot do. So, why would companies abide by such commitments? The answer lies, in part, in the changing social (and emerging legal) expectations that are now being placed on business. The 'rules of the game', to paraphrase Friedman, are changing and (some) companies are responding.

In most industries, large companies now rely on a global supply chain of contractors and suppliers. Nike, for example, sources its products from more than 550 factories, engaging one million workers across more than 40 countries.[28] In the mid-1990s, Nike faced allegations of using sweatshop labour to produce its goods in factories throughout Asia. Under a barrage of media criticism, Nike first denied that it had any responsibility for the factory working conditions, which allegedly included 'physical and verbal abuse of workers, hazardous working conditions, pennies per hour wages, and anti-union efforts throughout Indonesia, China, and Vietnam, where Nike employ[ed] over 350 000 workers'.[29] In response, and under pressure from unions, scholars and activists, Nike established a department tasked with working to improve factory conditions. Continuing criticism of the company led to protests on US college campuses, and in 1998, then CEO of Nike, Philip Knight, acknowledged that '[t]he Nike product has become synonymous with slave wages, forced overtime, and arbitrary abuse ... I truly believe the American consumer doesn't want to buy products made under abusive conditions'.[30] Today, Nike declares:

> [one of our] responsibilities as a global company is to play a role in bringing about positive, systemic change for workers within our supply chain and in the industry. We've run the course – from establishing a Code of Conduct ... to pulling together an internal team to enforce it ... and working with external bodies to monitor factories and work with stakeholders.[31]

No-one, including Nike, would argue that it is a company without human rights problems, but its first instinct is no longer to deny that it has a problem. One of the strategies Nike has pursued is to work collaboratively with its peers and a broader range of stakeholders in debating how to make changes that would move the needle beyond affecting only one group of workers in one factory. One of the features of the business and human rights movement since the late

1990s is the involvement of companies in voluntary multi-stakeholder governance initiatives as an attempt to curb corporate human rights abuses. The growth of such collaborations is largely a response to shortfalls in local labour laws and their enforcement in a global context.[32] These voluntary multi-stakeholder initiatives, which can include companies, civil society organisations such as trade unions and NGOs, and sometimes governments (though they are more frequently absent), have emerged to address the governance gaps that exist when companies operate in countries that cannot or will not fulfil their obligations to protect the rights of their own people.

Over the past two decades, these initiatives have burst forth from different business sectors – from telecommunications to apparel to private security contracting to palm oil – and appear to be an enduring feature in regulating global corporate conduct on human rights. Multi-stakeholder initiatives typically form in moments of crisis affecting a particular industry – situations in which corporations are under pressure to respond to public human rights allegations that no actor alone can effectively address. While the participation of civil society organisations can ostensibly result in more robust governance, their capacity to hold companies to account is arguably more limited as compared to the enforcement of legislation by the state.

The impact of the UN Guiding Principles on Business and Human Rights

The acceptance of the UN Guiding Principles by the UN Human Rights Council in 2011 was a significant step forward in bringing the idea of human rights in business circles into the mainstream. However, one of the common critiques of the UN Guiding Principles is that the broadly framed principles encourage, but do not oblige, companies to respect human rights.[33] They are not mandatory and are not 'law', but as we will see later, law also has its limitations. They are designed to provide guidance as to how the business world should integrate social concerns, such as protecting human rights and avoiding modern slavery, with economic ones. As guiding principles, they offer both companies and governments a way forward in incorporating human rights concerns into business decisions so that they are a core consideration rather than a peripheral afterthought. The UN Guiding Principles confirm that while governments have a legal obligation to protect human rights (as set out in international laws and adopted by national governments), companies also have a parallel and complementary responsibility to respect human rights. The UN Guiding Principle 15 defines this responsibility as companies having in place:

a a policy commitment to meet their responsibility to respect human rights;

b a human rights due-diligence process to identify, prevent, mitigate and account for how they address their impacts on human rights; and
c processes to enable the remediation of any adverse human rights impacts they cause or to which they contribute.

Companies have the potential to protect a wide array of internationally recognised human rights and their responsibility applies to all such rights, from avoiding slavery to allowing free speech. In practice, some human rights may be at greater risk from corporate activities than others, and therefore will be the focus of heightened attention. Modern slavery practices, which include situations where a worker may be deceptively recruited, forced or compelled to work, are an everyday reality for nearly 25 million workers. The basic tenets of workplace rights are set out in a litany of international human rights treaties established by the UN and the ILO. These treaties cover a wide range of rights including, but not only, the right to be free from slavery, the right to form trade unions, the right to free speech, the right to an adequate standard of living, women's rights, children's rights, and the rights of migrant workers. All the rights that are set out in treaties of the UN and the ILO are potentially relevant to companies. However, a key challenge is that international human rights law applies to states, not to other organisations such as businesses.

Therefore, we continue to rely on 'soft law' – non-binding principles agreed to voluntarily by businesses. The UN Guiding Principles offer a principled and pragmatic approach to incorporating human rights into business and human rights, and are distinct from the earlier CSR focus of some companies, which tended to highlight their philanthropic efforts as a way to counter criticism of their human rights record.[34] They establish a framework for how companies should behave and the top-down UN-curated guidance states that a company should avoid 'adverse human rights impacts'. Frameworks such as this can help us understand what businesses should and should not do and where we draw the line between a company directly violating someone's rights versus indirectly being linked to the problem.

Determining how a company affects human rights (and how to avoid adverse impacts) is a little more complicated than simply determining what rights might be potentially connected or relevant to a company's operations. According to the UN Guiding Principles, a company might be associated with 'adverse human rights impacts' by either 'causing, contributing or being directly linked' to them. In some cases, determining if a company causes adverse human rights impacts may be relatively straightforward.

For example, a company might engage in unsafe work practices that exposes its workers to hazardous chemicals without adequate personal protective equipment. In 2006, in a case that predated the establishment of

INTERNATIONAL HUMAN RIGHTS LAWS

The Universal Declaration of Human Rights (UDHR), adopted in 1948 by the UN, lists 30 substantive human rights that are promulgated as a common standard of achievement for all peoples and all nations: every 'individual and organ of society' shall strive by teaching and education to promote respect for these rights and, by progressive measures, secure their universal and effective recognition and observance. Motivated by the experiences of the two world wars, the UDHR was the first time that countries agreed on a comprehensive statement of inalienable human rights. As a declaration of the UN General Assembly, it does not itself create legal obligations. Nevertheless, the UDHR is frequently cited as the source of human rights obligations that corporations are urged to follow.

While the UDHR identifies human rights entitlements rather than explicit legal obligations, international human rights treaties transform those rights into binding legal obligations upon states (that is, governments). The International Covenant on Civil and Political Rights and the International Covenant on Economic, Social and Cultural Rights make all the rights in the UDHR, other than the right to property, obligations of states who are parties to them. Human rights obligations are also contained in subject-specific treaties including conventions of the ILO. The ILO has eight core conventions that cover subjects such as freedom of association and the right to organise, equality and non-discrimination, forced labour and child labour.

The laws of the UN and the ILO are adopted by governments and not directly enforceable against companies; however, the rights established in these laws are useful for understanding the spectrum of internationally recognised human rights that are potentially relevant to business. The state-centric framework of international human rights law emphasises the primary responsibility of governments to protect human rights while remaining partially oblivious to the opportunity to speak more directly to influential non-state actors including corporations. The size, revenues and global reach of some corporations now means that their potential power to affect communities is commensurate with those of states; yet they are not directly bound by international human rights laws. The resolution adopted by the UN Human Rights Council in 2014[35] to explore the development of a business and human rights treaty raises anew the issue of whether the international human rights law framework can accommodate corporate liability. While questions have been posed as to the necessity for a treaty, the potential effectiveness of a treaty and the theoretical and practical feasibility of establishing a framework to hold hundreds of thousands of corporations to account is an ongoing process, and one that acknowledges that there is a need for a global legal framework that directly addresses corporate violations of human rights.[36]

the UN Guiding Principles, a South African gold miner named Thembekile Mankayi sued AngloGold Ashanti, his former employer, stating that he developed the lung disease silicosis while working in the Vaal Reefs mine. He alleged that AngloGold Ashanti failed to meet its responsibility to provide its employees with a safe and healthy work environment. There was a long legal dispute between the parties as to whether Mr Mankayi could legally make such a claim, but on 3 March 2011, South Africa's highest court ruled in Mr Mankayi's favour. Mr Mankayi died of lung disease on 25 February 2011 before he could find out that the company could be held responsible for his illness.[37] In this case, the argument would be that the company caused the harm by failing to provide a safe working environment.

In other cases, where a company contributes to an adverse human rights impact, the company may not be directly causing the harm, but it may enable, incentivise or facilitate a third party's actions. For example, in 2007, long before the emergence of the UN Guiding Principles, US-based Yahoo! and its Chinese subsidiary were sued by two Chinese activists, who argued that the provision of information about their online activities by Yahoo! to Chinese law enforcement led to their arrest, a 10-year prison sentence and subsequent torture. The men had been accused by China of incitement to subvert state power and illegally providing state secrets to foreign entities. Mr Shi's alleged crime was an email he distributed via Yahoo!

advocating democratic reform and Mr Wang's was for another email he sent via Yahoo! that contained his comments on the restrictions on the media in covering the 15th anniversary of the Tiananmen Square uprising. Yahoo! ultimately settled the lawsuit and agreed to bear the plaintiffs' legal costs and establish a fund 'to provide humanitarian and legal aid to dissidents who have been imprisoned for expressing their views online'.[38] It was around this time that US-based technology companies, including Yahoo!, Google and Microsoft, found themselves in the firing line of a US congressional inquiry where Democrat Tom Lantos berated Yahoo! by infamously stating, 'while technologically and financially you are giants, morally you are pygmies'.[39] Here, while Yahoo! did not directly cause the harm, it is arguable that its actions contributed to subsequent human rights violations, and thus should assume some responsibility for remedying it.

Finally, the UN Guiding Principles suggest that a company still has some responsibility, even if it did not cause or contribute to the problem but is directly linked to the harm. For example, in 2018, Australia's ANZ Bank was accused of failing to meet its own human rights standards when it financed a Cambodian sugar plantation that was linked to human rights violations, including forced evictions, child labour and workplace injuries.[40] ANZ Bank was alleged to have lent tens of millions of dollars to Phnom Penh Sugar, through its Cambodian subsidiary, ANZ Royal Bank. The sugar company is said to have forced more than 1000 families off their land and engaged in exploitative work practices. While the bank did not itself engage in these practices, there is nevertheless a direct link between the operations, products and services of the bank and a so-called adverse human rights impact. A situation of 'direct linkage' may occur where a bank has provided finance to a client and the client, in the context of using this finance, acts in such a way that it causes the harm. Providing a financial product or service creates a business relationship between the bank and the client for the purposes of the UN Guiding Principles.

The UN Guiding Principles' broad framework has become a 'common reference point in the area of business and human rights'.[41] By more clearly delineating the relationship between a company and how it might affect human rights, the principles have moved human rights from a fringe CSR-coated philanthropic concern, to one that companies must address in their mainstream operations. A 2014 survey by *The Economist* (just three years after the UN endorsed the Guiding Principles) of 853 senior corporate executives found that 83 per cent of respondents agreed that human rights are a matter for business as well as governments.[42] However, the same survey revealed that '[w]hile corporate attitudes are evolving fairly quickly, concrete steps to reform company policies and to communicate such changes externally are slower to follow'.[43] That is, there is a delay translating principles into practice. This gets to the heart of some critiques of the UN Guiding Principles, which while acknowledging their useful synthesisation of human rights and business, their effective implementation and 'enforcement' is another (ongoing) debate. The question remains: if such initiatives and the development of the broadly framed principles encourage, but do not oblige, companies to respect human rights, is this enough? Some companies and sectors are more resistant than others to change, so the question becomes: what is the best way to get companies to 'walk the talk'?

The more things change, the more they stay the same

On 24 April 2013, an eight-storey factory building – Rana Plaza – collapsed in the industrial outskirts of Dhaka, the capital of Bangladesh, killing more than 1100 garment workers and seriously injuring hundreds more. This disaster came almost 30 years after several thousand people died in Bhopal, India, when an accident at the Union Carbide pesticide plant released at least 30 tonnes of a highly toxic gas.

> The pesticide plant was surrounded by shanty towns, leading to more than 600 000 people being exposed to the deadly gas cloud that night. The gases stayed low to the ground, causing victims' throats and eyes to burn, inducing nausea, and many deaths. Estimates of the death toll vary

> from as few as 3800 to as many as 16 000, but government figures now refer to an estimate of 15 000 killed over the years.[44]

In the intervening years, between the disasters in Bhopal and Dhaka, the UN Guiding Principles were adopted, the OECD and ILO disseminated their standards, companies joined multi-stakeholder initiatives, and still tragedy struck. The deaths of more than 1100 workers in Bangladesh dominated global headlines for a few weeks, but the public's attention eventually waned. The collapse of the Rana Plaza building illustrated, in stark detail, the poor conditions in Bangladesh's garment factories and the complex problems inherent in a global production system that relies on remote supply chains. Thirty years ago in Bangladesh there were fewer than 400 garment factories employing about 120 000 workers.[45] Today, there are estimated to be more than 4000 factories[46] with more than four million workers.[47]

These jobs have lifted many people out of the destitute poverty that village life might otherwise offer them, and while there is no doubt that the garment business has been a driving force for social development in Bangladesh, it is also true that industrialisation has come with significant costs, especially for the health, safety and wellbeing of workers. When the Rana Plaza building collapsed, attention quickly turned to the global companies who were sourcing their clothing from these factories. Companies such as the Italian fashion brand

Benetton, the Spanish chain Mango, the UK retailer Primark and the US-based J.C. Penney were all linked to the garment factories in Rana Plaza. Benetton's initial reaction to the disaster was to dispute it was involved in any of factories in the collapsed building and the company issued a forceful denial.[48] Five days later, as public attention intensified and photos emerged of garments in the rubble with the Benetton label, the company admitted that it had a one-time order from a supplier in Rana Plaza, but claimed the manufacturer had been removed from its approved supplier list.

Benetton's initial handling of the aftermath was clumsy and indicative of the company's desire to waive responsibility. As the garment industry has developed in Bangladesh, local manufacturers and global brands have come to rely on a system of extensive subcontracting that is pervasive throughout the supply chain. Subcontracting is often conducted in a manner that is not fully transparent to buyers or regulators. It has become an essential feature of the garment sector in Bangladesh to increase margins and boost production capacity while keeping costs low. While parts of an order for jeans might be assembled in a brand-authorised factory in Dhaka, other components may be subcontracted to another 'unauthorised' factory in order to meet the timeline imposed by the brand. There are many steps that precede the sewing of the jeans, including the sourcing of cotton, dyeing of the material and preparation of the zipper to name a few. This back end of the supply chain is not always visible to the buyer and more difficult to ascertain. The ad hoc growth of the garment sector in Bangladesh over the last 30 years is a quintessential example of weak rule of law coupled with strong business opportunities. But lax regulation across the sector created serious risks that led to the Rana Plaza disaster, which both governments and business bear responsibility for. The death of more than 1100 workers exposed the dark side of globalisation and is emblematic of a long history of broader human rights abuses perpetuated in supply chains across a multitude of sectors and countries. Workplaces that utilise modern slavery are generally a hotbed of other human rights abuses, which have either failed to be detected or failed to be redressed. Abusive workplaces tend to operate on a continuum of exploitation.

'Modern slavery' is the current buzzword, but research shows that if labour abuses such as 'non-payment of minimum wage, unfair dismissals, forced and unpaid overtime, denial of benefits, and denial of the rights of freedom of association and collective bargaining are prevalent and left unchecked, more severe exploitation often develops'.[49] While the scale of death and injury toll from the Rana Plaza disaster was exceptional, it is an accurate barometer of the endemic problems that exist more broadly across global supply chains. On 11 September 2012, a fire in the Ali Enterprises garment factory in Karachi, Pakistan, killed nearly 300 workers. On 24 November 2012, a factory fire at

Tazreen Fashions Limited in Dhaka killed 117 workers. A 2018 study by Sheffield University of 22 tea plantations in India (including those producing for Fairtrade) found that workers faced widespread sexual harassment, suffered beatings and had wages and benefits withheld.[50] All of these workplaces had been inspected by auditors and approved for production for global companies.

The imperfect reality is that many goods, particularly but not only consumer products such as clothing, toys and electronics, are manufactured in countries, both developed and developing, where governments do not sufficiently protect the rights of workers, and business is left to pick up the slack. History demonstrates that business has a knack for exploiting poorly regulated workplaces. Weak labour practices are also endemic in service industries, and workers in the construction and domestic service sectors have been found to be working as modern-day slaves. They are recruited in one country for a job in another that bears little relationship to the work and pay rates they were promised. Global governance regimes and governments are simply not up to the task of protecting workers, and it is logical and necessary that some of this responsibility must now more squarely fall on business.

A business case for human rights

What is abundantly clear is that companies are regularly confronted with human rights issues in their day-to-day operations. Not all will be classified as modern slavery, but all are problematic. Whether it is an IT company ignoring privacy concerns or a manufacturing company using forced labour in its supply chain, human rights are relevant to a company's core business processes, no matter if it is operating in Sydney, Shenzhen, Seattle or Sialkot. For many companies, not addressing these issues is no longer an option. However, while attention is more commonly focused on consumer-facing global brands, there are myriad small- and medium-sized businesses, especially those operating in predominantly non-English-speaking countries, that fall under the radar. While most people are aware of Google, the world's best-known internet search engine, there is far less awareness (outside China) of Baidu, a Chinese-based search engine (with 800 million active monthly users), which was the lowest ranked internet company in the list compiled by the Ranking Digital Rights group in 2017 in its human rights benchmarking exercise.[51]

Likewise, many consumers are well aware of the consistent pattern of human rights violations alleged against Shell in relation to its decades-old operations in Nigeria, but they are unlikely to be so familiar with the more than 130 Australian companies operating in 34 countries across Africa, making Australia the largest international miner on the continent.[52] A 2015 report by the International Consortium of Investigative Journalists found that since 2004, more than 380 people have died in mining accidents or off-site skirmishes connected to Australian companies in Africa.[53] These companies are not well-known household brands and face minimal public scrutiny, but nevertheless they may have a direct and adverse effect on the communities in which they operate. The question is how to motivate all companies, those in the public eye and those that are not, to operate in a manner that respects human rights? Beyond the imperative that exists by reference to international guidelines, how can corporations make the business case for human rights and explain to their shareholders and stakeholders why changes, even costly changes, are beneficial to their businesses?

The first question might be whether we need a 'business case'. Fundamental human rights standards are universal imperatives. Legally, international laws on human rights, which have been established in laws over the last 60 years, bind governments not companies, but their widespread acceptance as universal standards and the need for companies to adhere to basic concepts of workers' dignity may be sufficient rationale for why businesses ought to support basic rights. A recent study analysed how employees could most effectively get management onboard with support for social issues.[54] It showed that the moral case that framed the social issue as part of the organisation's values and mission was likely to be the most successful. Yet in practical situations – including building consensus and traction within a company – it may also be useful to be able to articulate, in commercially relevant ways, why it is important to adopt a proactive approach to identifying, preventing and remedying human rights risks.

What then is the 'business case', beyond just the powerful but rather general contemporary management idea of 'doing well by doing good'? It is about doing what is *right*, not just what may be seen as *good*: thus now-familiar ideas about CSR and corporate philanthropy should be distinguished from business and human rights. These days the business and human rights discussion should include an understanding of global standards (like those, but not limited to those, set out in the UN Guiding Principles) that reflect an international consensus and recognition that companies have a responsibility to respect human rights. This responsibility should not be considered optional. Proactive, consistent and systematic respect for human rights is a long-term imperative that aligns with two basic business concepts.

First, concern for preventing human rights abuses should be part of a larger risk management strategy. It is a basic tenet of business, consistent with Friedman's mantra of generating profits, that companies should minimise legal, regulatory, financial, reputational and other risks that might devalue business operations.

The second is a focus on brand-building that is more, but not exclusively, relevant to consumer-facing companies. All businesses should maximise the scope for attracting and retaining ethically-minded consumers, investors and employees. Paul Polman, former CEO of Unilever, a company ranked 163 in the 2018 Fortune 500 company rankings (and best known through its brands including Dove, Lipton, Lux and Rexona) went on the record to argue:

> with governments being gridlocked, the need for change increasingly has to come from responsible business. If business understands that, they'll have a bright future. If businesses don't understand that, I think the consumer will increasingly vote them out of business.[55]

It 'remains an open question as to whether the relative costs and economic benefits of adopting strong human rights policies can be quantified'[56] but there are examples of where companies have incurred costs because of a failure to adhere to human rights standards.[57] Even where formal legal consequences may not arise, businesses may be seen as accountable in various ways to the market, financiers and insurers, consumers and others. But the fact is, that while there are now thousands of companies around the world that both profess and act on concerns about human rights, workplace abuses are still a reality for many workers. While guidelines continue to proliferate, and companies are both cajoled and coerced into responding to human rights concerns, there is a growing frustration with companies continuing to treat human rights as an optional extra. This has given rise to a movement to harden human rights expectations by legally mandating corporate behaviour that incorporates respect for international human rights standards, whether in the form of an international treaty or in domestic laws, such as the UK's or Australia's *Modern Slavery Act*.

There has long been a tug of war between scholars, activists, companies, unions, governments and others about the value of 'law' as a mechanism to cross-pollinate business with human rights. Law is but one way to influence behaviour and not all laws are created or implemented equally. Some laws (such as some of the recent efforts to target modern slavery) are created without any in-built mechanism to ensure compliance, and so are of limited value. At present in the UK and Australia, the failure of a company to meet a tax obligation may result in a penalty being applied, but the failure of a company to meet its reporting requirements under the UK or Australian Modern Slavery Act does not. There are also other challenges in regulating global concerns about human rights via legislation.

Laws most commonly operate within national borders, but companies do not. To date, legal efforts to regulate human rights abuses across global supply chains have been limited. Government laws in a so-called 'host country' (for example, the country where the goods are produced) will generally target local conduct and likely have limited effectiveness in holding a global corporation (which is headquartered in another country) to account for the activities of its suppliers in a host country.[58]

For example, in June 2013, following the collapse of the Rana Plaza building, the Bangladeshi Parliament passed a legislative reform package that focused on local issues, such as improving labour laws about union representation, but did not address broader supply chain regulation. However, law (generally) is now being touted and more seriously considered as a potential mechanism to regulate global supply chains and in particular, modern slavery. The UK, France, the US, Australia, the Netherlands, Canada, Germany and Switzerland are just some of the countries using or proposing new laws to combat corporate irresponsibility in global supply chains. Some of these focus on modern slavery, some are broader and try to capture a wide range of human rights violations. Alongside these emerging legal initiatives are a range of voluntary guidelines and tactics used at both local and global levels to address the broader human rights abuses that exist in global supply chains.

Accepting that rights must be respected by corporations, wherever in the world they operate, is one thing; making it happen is quite another. To date, attempts to hold business accountable for complying with human rights standards has relied on a patchwork system of protection, which combines myriad soft guidelines, lawsuits and ad hoc naming and shaming tactics used by NGOs. In practical terms, non-state (or non-government) actors – such as unions, human rights activists, workers, consumers and scholars – have either deliberately or by default assumed the role of motivating companies to respect rights throughout their global operations, often in the absence of effective government enforcement. With the emergence of recent laws targeting modern slavery in global supply chains, (some) governments are stepping back into the regulatory framework and asserting their right to regulate. In the interim, these non-state actors have both been filling a regulatory lacuna and building capacity for governments to get back into the game and institutionalise the norms that have been steadily established by practice in recent decades. As will be discussed in chapter 4, the law has a place, but it is most likely going to have to be a joint regulatory effort to significantly move the needle in improving working conditions in the world's many and varied corporate supply chains.

4

Regulating the business of modern slavery: Law, what is it good for?

Modern slavery's presence in corporate supply chains is a reality, but to many of us, including the companies that rely on it, it remains an abstract concept. Something remote that exists beyond our control. An invisible evil associated with global markets that is impossible to regulate. But from the moment you get out of bed in the morning to the time you go to sleep, there is a strong chance that the products you use and the services you rely on are linked to modern slavery and because of that connection, we all assume some level of responsibility and (potential) control over it.[1]

Let's take a typical morning routine as an example. You wake up in the morning and take a shower. Palm oil is a common ingredient in household soap and is probably in the one you just used. The vast majority of the world's palm oil supply, nearly 85 per cent, is grown in Indonesia and Malaysia, and to meet the growing global demand for cheaply produced palm oil, some producers are relying on modern slavery. On your way to work, you stop for a cappuccino with a sprinkling of chocolate on top. Your coffee may contain beans that were harvested and cultivated by slaves in Côte d'Ivoire. Côte d'Ivoire, together with Ghana, produces 60 per cent of the world's cocoa. From the cocoa bean to the chocolate that sits on a supermarket shelf, the cocoa supply chain is difficult to trace and it is often not clear how the cocoa in any particular product is sourced. An estimated 95 per cent of retail chocolate today is not certified to be free from child or forced labour.[2] The fruit you snack on may have been picked in Australia by migrant workers who were lured to Australia with the promise of high incomes and now work for a pittance and are trapped in debt bondage. A 2017 study found that large-scale wage theft is prevalent across a range of industries in Australia, but the worst paid jobs were in fruit and vegetable picking and farm work. Almost one in seven of those surveyed working in these sectors earned $5 per hour or less.[3] Your day has only just begun, and you are already intimately connected with modern slavery.

It is increasingly apparent that the decades spent by activists and policymakers in pursuing corporate self-regulation to 'take care' of the human rights problems in supply chains has not resulted in a problem-free chain of production. As a response to the lack of global enforcement of labour standards, some countries are developing laws to try and regulate global supply chains. Whether making new laws is an effective way of tackling the problem, and what other opportunities there are for leveraging change in supply chains, is an open question. What is clear is that right now, pressure is mounting on business to do more to address modern slavery and new laws are being developed to say it is no longer enough to allow the complexity of global supply chains to prevent business from at least identifying risks.

In order to address the problem, it is a useful first step to expose the issues. New laws are demanding greater transparency about how and where our clothes, phones, carpets, coffee and bricks are sourced and produced. Earlier chapters examined some of the drivers that are placing pressure on companies to address modern slavery and human rights issues more generally and the limitations of relying solely on voluntary efforts to do so. This chapter briefly recaps some of the regulatory efforts that preceded these new laws and then looks more closely at what legal strategies are currently being used to expose and reduce modern slavery, and how companies should respond. The first disclosure law that focused on modern slavery, the *Transparency in Supply Chains Act*, was passed in California in 2010. In 2015, the UK passed its *Modern Slavery Act*, and Australia passed its own law in 2018. With more than 40 million people in slavery around the world, and an estimated nearly 25 million of these being workers enduring forced labour, this means there are a lot of companies (and consumers) relying on slaves. Modern slavery is a reality. The question is, what is being done to reduce it and will it be effective? Will forcing companies to be more transparent about how and where they produce their products lead to better labour conditions throughout the entire supply chain? And if not, what else is needed?

The need for a different approach

In 1973, the United Natiuons (UN) Economic and Social Council pulled together an expert group for the task of developing a global framework for holding business to account for human rights violations. In 1974, the UN established the Centre on Transnational Corporations; by 1977, it was coordinating the negotiation of the Draft Code of Conduct on Transnational Corporations. The text of the Draft Code contained duties for companies to respect host countries' development goals, observe their domestic laws, respect fundamental human rights, and observe consumer and environmental protection objectives. The Draft Code was never officially adopted, its legal nature was never established, and the Centre was eventually disbanded. Whether the code should be legally binding or voluntary in nature was debated, with proponents on both sides. If binding, the Draft Code would have served as a treaty with both national and international mechanisms for implementation. If voluntary, it would have served as a set of broad guidelines to be observed by participating parties. Around the same time, the Organisation for Economic Co-operation and Development (OECD) was developing its own recommendations to advise governments and business on what responsible business conduct looks like. Another attempt was made in the 1990s to develop a UN-based framework for corporate accountability, but this also failed. The UN Guiding Principles on Business and Human Rights, adopted by the UN in 2011, now provide a basis for a broad, global, soft-law (that is, not legally binding) framework for establishing corporate responsibility for human rights. This stands in contrast to ongoing discussions at the UN to develop a global, legally binding treaty to regulate business with respect to human rights.

The modern slavery laws that are now emerging in places such as the UK and Australia are piggybacking on years of earlier, broader initiatives claiming to address the impacts of the rapid pace of globalisation and its negative effects on working conditions in supplier factories, often located in developing countries. Many of these earlier initiatives were characterised as embodying strong elements of corporate self-regulation and relied heavily on corporate codes of conduct (voluntary standards that are often loosely based on international labour standards) to regulate behaviour. These codes were sometimes developed with limited stakeholder

APPLE AND ITS SUPPLY CHAIN WORKERS

The public criticism and media attention that forced apparel and footwear companies to act in the 1990s has more recently focused in on one of the world's giants in the electronics sector – Apple – and the working conditions in its supplier factories in Asia. In the last decade, Apple has become one of the richest and most successful companies in the world, in part by mastering global manufacturing. However, a series of media and NGO reports highlighted allegations that factory workers employed by Foxconn (a principal but not exclusive supplier for Apple) assembled iPhones, iPads and other devices while working in onerous and sometimes unsafe work environments.[4] One report argued:

> [e]mployees work excessive overtime, in some cases seven days a week, and live in crowded dorms. Some say they stand so long that their legs swell until they can hardly walk. Under-age workers have helped build Apple's products, and the company's suppliers have improperly disposed of hazardous waste and falsified records.[5]

In 2010, 18 employees at Foxconn plants in China were reported to have attempted suicide, resulting in 14 deaths. The suicides drew media scrutiny and garnered significant negative attention for both Apple and Foxconn and, to a lesser extent, other global electronic brands also producing in those factories.[6] Foxconn is a major manufacturer that also produces goods for companies such as Dell, HP, Motorola, Nintendo, Nokia, and Sony. Employment practices at Foxconn were investigated by several of its customers, including Apple and HP. Like Nike before it, Apple took a closer look at its supplier code of conduct (first made publicly available in 2005) and the mechanisms designed to monitor workplace conditions.

In 2009, Apple made debt-bonded labour (which can be a form of modern slavery) a core violation of its Apple Supplier Code of Conduct and limited any recruitment fees paid by the worker to one month's wages. Debt-bonded labour occurs when a person is required to work in exchange for the repayment of a debt or other obligation, which may include a 'recruitment fee' paid by the worker in order to get the job. In 2012, Apple decided to join a multi-stakeholder initiative – the Fair Labour Association (FLA) – in an effort to improve its factory-auditing process, but this did little to stem criticism of its production processes or provide sufficient comfort to those who were investigating its supply chain. Apple has since left the FLA.

A holistic appraisal of Apple's supply chain will conclude that (like most large companies) there remain real issues with the working conditions in its supplier factories. However, the company has taken on a leadership role in the electronics sector on one issue and has proved effective in instigating change. In 2015, to prevent workers becoming indentured labourers, Apple mandated that workers should not pay any recruitment fees to get a job, even if such fees were legal in the workers' country of origin. In Apple's 'Supplier Responsibility 2019 Progress Report' it reported that, in the previous year, it required its suppliers to repay US$616 000 in recruitment fees to 287 of the suppliers' employees. It reported suppliers have returned US$30.9 million in recruitment fees to workers since 2008.[7]

input and few, if any, included independent or transparent monitoring and reporting mechanisms to assess compliance with international human rights and labour and environmental standards.

The reasons that the various codes, guidelines and principles have proliferated in the last three to four decades are multifaceted (including an increase in pressure on companies from NGOs and a willingness on the part of some companies to adapt corporate strategies to incorporate such codes), but it is clear that the development of these initiatives is, in part, a response to an inadequate legal framework. Unsurprisingly, these modes of corporate self-governance that emerged in force in the 1990s and continue today have been criticised for their lack of robustness, legitimacy and effectiveness.[8] Such critiques have influenced some companies to engage more fully with external stakeholders and join multi-stakeholder initiatives to develop and implement compliance with human rights.

Ad hoc efforts are a marker for how the corporate social responsibility (CSR) and business and human rights movements have evolved over a number of years. Some giant steps forward, accompanied by some steps back, and specific progress is often contingent on a response to a media exposé highlighting issues such as child labour, forced labour, long hours, low pay or unsafe working conditions in a company's supply chain. The push and pull between global versus local and between voluntary versus mandatory efforts to regulate corporate impacts on business and human rights does not offer clear black and white distinctions, but rather shades of grey. How do top-down guidelines issued by the UN or the OECD filter down to affect workers' rights on the floor of a subcontracting factory in Bangladesh? To some, the loose language of corporate responsibility rather than obligation implies an acceptance of a 'world where companies are encouraged, but not obliged, to respect human rights'[9] and requires few real changes in the way business operates. It is possible that 'the soothing promise of responsibility can deflect public attention from the need for stricter laws and regulations'.[10] Responsibility is distinguished from accountability, and corporations interpreting these principles in practice may choose to take their cue (or not) from a mix of international standards selectively embodied in various guidelines or declarations.

It is reasonable to argue that these codes, guidelines and principles have emerged simply because there is a lack of anything better and/or as a tactic for avoiding government regulation. But the use of this type of 'soft law' can also be a deliberate strategic choice – made by business and sometimes other stakeholders – because it is more likely to attract participation or buy-in from a broad group of stakeholders (including business and government). The attraction of relying on a soft-law approach can be easily understood if the standards are viewed as containing aspirational goals that aim for the best possible scenario with limited constraints if such goals are not met. However, soft law is not always commensurate with soft results, and so-called 'hard law' (treaties or domestic laws that are legally binding) may not always deliver either. Any clear demarcation between hard and soft law is challenging and while some may argue that 'the essence of any soft law rule is that it is not binding'[11] in this particular field, differentiation between soft and hard law is not binary but should be viewed as a continuum. What is legally sanctioned is distinguishable from what is not, but reputational sanctions can be crucial to business.[12] The reality is that both law and 'not-law' are only as strong as their enforcement capacity, but their potential normative value, in shaping corporate and public culture as to what is and is not expected of companies in overseeing their supply chains, is also important.

The emergence of new transparency laws

Increased public disclosure of human rights standards in corporate supply chains is quickly becoming an expectation of companies and, in some countries, it is not just expected, but required. What began primarily as a social expectation is slowly becoming a legal norm. Led by the development of new legal social disclosure requirements in places such as the UK, the US (in particular California), France and Australia, companies are now required to be more transparent about working conditions in their supply chains. This regulatory strategy reflects a growing consensus that both government and business have a role to play in addressing the human rights impacts of business, and that government must step into the global framework and regulate it. Some laws, such as those in the UK, California and Australia, are specifically focused on corporate reporting as a means of reducing modern slavery. Others, such as the 'duty of vigilance' law passed in France in 2017, are broader and incorporate human rights risks more generally, imposing additional requirements on companies beyond increased transparency about supply chain working conditions. Since 2010, at least 11 national or regional laws have been approved, or are under consideration that require companies to report on their supply chain practices.[13] What is less clear is whether these disclosure requirements are sufficient to generate real changes in the lives of workers who are working as modern-day slaves.

California's *Transparency in Supply Chains Act* (S.B. 657) was adopted in 2010 and came into effect in 2012.[14] It was followed by the UK's *Modern Slavery Act* of 2015 and Australia's *Modern Slavery Act* of 2018. Each of these laws follows a basic model that requires companies to report on the risks of modern slavery in their supply chains. The California Act requires all retailers and manufacturers (with global annual gross receipts of US$100 million) that 'do business' in California to disclose on their websites any action they are taking to 'eradicate slavery and human trafficking from its direct supply chain for tangible goods for sale'. The required disclosures are to be posted on the company's website with a 'conspicuous and easily understood link' to the required information on the website's home page. While the Californian law does not impose a penalty on companies for not complying with the law, such laws can be the genesis for other legal actions.

	California *Transparency in Supply Chains Act 2010*	**UK** *Modern Slavery Act 2015*	**Australia** *Modern Slavery Act 2018*	**France** *Duty of Vigilance Law 2017*
Coverage	Retail sellers and manufacturers doing business in California with annual worldwide receipts that exceed US$100 million (approximately 3000–4000 firms).	Entities with revenue over £36 million (approximately 12 000).	Entities with revenue over AU$100 million (including the Australian Government) (approximately 3000).	French companies that have more than 5000 employees domestically or employ 10 000 employees or more worldwide (approximately 250).
Scope	Focuses on their direct suppliers.	Government guidance encourages companies to take a commonsense approach with supply chains, given its 'everyday meaning'.	Government guidance urges entities to monitor modern slavery risks in their global operations and supply chains, not just their operations and supply chains in Australia.	Includes parent company, companies it controls directly or indirectly and subcontractors and suppliers with whom it maintains an 'established business relationship'.

	California *Transparency in Supply Chains Act 2010*	**UK** *Modern Slavery Act 2015*	**Australia** *Modern Slavery Act 2018*	**France** *Duty of Vigilance Law 2017*
eporting equirement	Disclose the extent they engage in: - verification - auditing - certification - internal accountability and policies - training. Companies have the option of submitting a 'no action taken' disclosure.	Disclose in a statement on their websites to 'what extent, if any' they have: - an organisational structure, business model and supply chain relationships - policies in relation to slavery and human trafficking - due diligence processes - risk identification and assessment - assessment of effectiveness of actions - training.	Mandated disclosures include: - structure, operations and supply chains - modern slavery risks - actions taken to assess and address modern slavery risks - assessment of effectiveness of actions - consultation process.	Make their vigilance plans and report on: - risk assessment of company and subsidiaries and subcontractors - actions to mitigate identified risks or prevent serious violations - mechanisms to alert the company to risks and collect signals of potential or actual risk - assessment of effectiveness of actions.
ue iligence	Not directly required	Not directly required	Not directly required but referred to in actions taken to address risks	Required

	California *Transparency in Supply Chains Act 2010*	**UK** *Modern Slavery Act 2015*	**Australia** *Modern Slavery Act 2018*	**France** *Duty of Vigilance Law 2017*
Compliance mechanism	Market pressure, i.e. businesses who comply will enjoy reputational benefits and vice versa (no punitive measures). The duty to issue a statement is enforceable by the California Attorney General through an injunction.	Market pressure, i.e. businesses who comply will enjoy reputational benefits and vice versa (no punitive measures). The duty to issue a statement is enforceable by the secretary of state through an injunction.	Market pressure, i.e. businesses who comply will enjoy reputational benefits and vice versa (no punitive measures). Section 16A introduces a 'comply or explain' provision, enabling the relevant minister to identify the non-compliant entity.	Civil recourse (punitive) Any concerned party has standing to request that a judge compel a company to establish, implement or publish a vigilance plan. Companies could be subject to liability if individuals are harmed by a company's failure to establish or implement a plan.

LAWSUITS TARGETING CORPORATE SUPPLY CHAINS

In August 2015, two separate lawsuits, one filed against Costco (*Sud v. Costco Wholesale Corporation* (2017)) and the other against Nestlé (*Melanie Barber et al., Plaintiffs v. Nestlé USA, Inc., a Delaware Corporation; and Nestlé Purina Petcare Co., a Missouri Corporation, Defendants* (2015)), alleged the use of slave labour in their corporate supply chains to import seafood products into the US. The Costco and Nestlé lawsuits relied on a combination of longstanding unfair business practices laws and consumer protection laws, combined with the California *Transparency in Supply Chains Act*. The separate lawsuits alleged that various public disclosures by both Costco and Nestlé were fraudulent and misleading, because while the companies state that they do not tolerate human trafficking and slavery in their supply chain, they continue to sell seafood products that are allegedly the result of slave labour.

In its 2015 *Trafficking in Persons Report* examining human trafficking in 188 countries, the US State Department cited concerns about slave labour in Thailand's fishing industry and criticised the Thai government's record in fighting exploitation.[15] Some of the practices alleged to be occurring in the Thai fishing industry include torture, chaining of workers and killing of those who seek to escape illegal fishing vessels. Neither Costco nor Nestlé was accused of engaging directly in such practices, but of working with companies in their supply chains that were sourcing seafood from suppliers who do engage in such practices.

Both lawsuits were subsequently dismissed. In the Costco case, the court ruled that the plaintiffs failed to establish that the world's second largest retail chain was bound to inform customers that modern-day slavery could be part of its supply chain. The court noted that while the facts described were 'tragic and "raise significant ethical concerns"'[16] the plaintiffs failed to show that Costco had a duty to disclose the information about labour abuses in the supply chain on its product packaging. Separately, the Nestlé case was dismissed because the court found that the California *Transparency in Supply Chains Act* provides companies with a safe harbour. This means that a company only has to disclose the efforts it is making to prevent forced labour, and it is not obligated to disclose the actual risk of forced labour in its supply chain.

Further lawsuits have been pursued against companies demanding more disclosure. In a 2018 decision by a Californian court (*Hodson v. Mars, Inc* (2018)) the court held the company did not have a duty to disclose the use of slave labour in its cocoa supply chain on its product labels because 'they are not physical defects that affect the central function of the chocolate products'.[17] Another lawsuit against Nestlé (*Doe v. Nestlé* (2018)) regarding its alleged use of slave labour in its cocoa supply chain continues in the US.

To prevent being targeted in such cases, and/or in preparation for defeating one, companies should be able to demonstrate reasonable and good-faith control and monitoring of their supply chains. Perfect supply chain compliance with human rights policies and goals may not be able to be proven (and may not be achievable), but being able to show that a company implemented robust procedures, engaged in diligent efforts to follow and enforce those procedures, and monitored regularly will be important. However, such efforts are not directly required under the Californian law.

A 2019 UK Supreme Court decision in *Vedanta Resources PLC and another v Lungowe and others* ([2019] UKSC 20) examined whether the company might owe a duty of care to communities harmed as a result of pollution caused by mining activities of its Zambian subsidiary. Although not dealing with supply chain questions, the court suggested such a duty might be owed if the parent company (Vedanta) sufficiently intervened in the management of the mine and one such indicator might be found in the public disclosures made by Vedanta in its sustainability reports [para. 53], suggesting transparency requirements may one day open the door a little to more concrete legal liability. Innovative law suits are starting to put companies on notice about their supply chain obligations, but the extent of their legal liability for harm done to workers in their supply chains remains unclear.

The UK *Modern Slavery Act*, passed into law in 2015, works on a similar model to the Californian law. It was the first national law to use the term 'modern slavery' and gave it global resonance. The law defines modern slavery to include 'slavery, servitude and forced or compulsory labour' and 'human trafficking'. Section 54 of the Act requires any commercial organisation that supplies goods or services, carries on business or part of a business in the UK, and whose annual turnover is £36 million or more (estimated to be more than 12 000 companies[18]), to produce an annual modern slavery statement on steps taken to assess and manage the risk of slavery and human trafficking. Statements must be published on the company's website, with a link to the statement in a prominent place on that website's home page. Statements must be approved by the board of directors, elevating human rights concerns to board level. The UK Act was established with the aim of abolishing modern slavery in the UK following a 2013 government estimate that there are between 10 000 and 13 000 potential victims of modern slavery in the country, and media stories were coming to light about the plight of workers in the UK.[19]

The question is whether these new types of transparency laws are, or will be, effective in reducing modern slavery. Kate Roberts, of the Human Trafficking Foundation in the UK, points out, 'The [UK] Act has done a lot to raise awareness. Unfortunately, in practice, we're still waiting to really see many tangible outcomes from

THE UK'S HIDDEN PROBLEM

In 2012, a group of six Lithuanian workers were recruited to come to the UK to work in the food industry.[20] Upon arrival, their visas were taken from them and they were forced to live in a small, squalid home with mattresses that were infected with bed bugs. Their work involved catching chickens in order to supply eggs for retailers and restaurants across the UK, such as the major brand Happy Eggs.[21] Between being transported to various farms on journeys longer than seven hours, they were forced to sleep on a minibus. They were charged excessive recruitment fees without receiving adequate pay, and they were not given any decent facilities to wash, rest, eat or drink.[22] In 2016, the UK High Court ruled in favour of the men and the company paid more than £1 million in compensation to the workers.[23] A subsequent case decided in 2019 also found in favour of more of the trafficked workers.[24]

In a case from 2004,[25] a group of Polish workers were also brought to work in the UK in a chicken-packaging factory. The factory was one of many subcontractors in Sainsbury's supply chain. The workers were housed in a room with no furniture and with piles of rubbish and used syringes. They worked 18-hour shifts between the hours of 2am to 10pm and were threatened with eviction and loss of pay if they complained or tried to seek help. The workers were unable to register with the UK Home Office and this put them at the additional risk of working illegally. Ultimately, it was with the involvement of a workers' union that they were able to escape.

it yet'.[26] Early analysis of the Californian Act and the UK *Modern Slavery Act* indicates a tendency towards the production of corporate reports that minimally meet the procedural 'tick the box' requirements of the laws. Year-on-year analysis of compliance with the Californian Act shows some slight improvement with compliance requirements, but still indicates that 48 per cent of companies are not complying with the basic disclosure requirements of the law.[27] Another study concluded that 'analysis of the extensiveness of the disclosure suggests that, overall, the responses tend to be more symbolic than substantive'.[28] While select corporate statements (for example, Marks & Spencer) have been praised as providing useful information, more generally the law has engendered a corporate response that falls short of any serious effort to address modern slavery in their supply chains.[29]

In 2018, several big-name British retailers, including Marks & Spencer, Tesco and the Co-op, called on the UK government to strengthen the law. They believe that corporate compliance with the Act has been 'weak' due to a lack of unification and enforcement.[30] This call to action is acknowledgment that for such laws to work, they must be uniformly adopted, not just by a few companies. Monitoring and improving working conditions in supply chains costs money, and the law must be enforced broadly to even the playing field. Because of the diversity of companies that may source their clothing from a single factory in Bangladesh, it is imperative that all companies in that supply chain are acting to reduce modern slavery and other human rights abuses, not just those who are more likely to face reputational consequences if they fail to act.

With both the Californian and UK laws, there is no central repository where the corporate statements are held, and in the UK there is no official public list detailing which companies need to report. The Business & Human Rights Centre, a non-governmental organisation, does host an online repository for statements. The Californian law only requires companies to report once to be in compliance, rather than mandating annual transparency reports. Compliance with these laws largely depends on the pressure exerted by external parties – consumers, investors, civil society – to induce compliance. The assumption in these laws, known as social disclosure laws, is that the transparency gained from disclosure will incentivise corporate action to address human rights risks. There are several problems with this assumption.

The first is that it relies on meaningful disclosure. That is, verifiable information that allows the public to make an assessment of the company's efforts to eradicate slave labour. However, companies are not always reporting on issues that matter the most. To date, many corporate statements on modern slavery report on things like general philanthropic activities, the scope of their corporate policies and their relationships with only their first-tier suppliers. What companies should be reporting on is the specific risks of modern slavery relevant to their products. For example, a recent study of global tea supply chains found that 'key indicators of vulnerability to forced labour in the tea industry include: the underpayment of workers by tea producers; tea producers' under-provision of services for workers' basic needs like electricity, water, and toilets; and debt bondage amongst workers at the base of their supply chains'.[31] The study argues that the 2016/2017 modern slavery statement by Tata Global Beverages GB Limited (who manufacture Tetley branded tea) focuses on relevant policies within its Code of Conduct; participation in private certification schemes and partnerships; and training, but not on any of the key indicators that would provide a more accurate assessment of modern slavery risks. The information disclosed by the company is not meaningful in assessing the risks of modern slavery.

Secondly, the social disclosure laws assume active participation of consumers as regulators of the law. That is, if we as consumers know that the fish we eat was harvested by slaves, then we will be less likely to buy it, which will force the company to change its practices. However, sole reliance on the ethical consumer to police corporate supply chains for modern slavery depends in part of the veracity and accessibility of information available to consumers and also relies on consumers to 'put their money where their mouth is'. Some studies indicate that consumers are not always willing to deploy their purchasing power in this manner, and reliance on consumers as regulators is sometimes referred to as the 'myth of the ethical consumer'.[32] This tactic of consumer policing is also likely to be restricted to those companies that are primarily consumer-facing or brand-dependent, and will not be as effective against the multitude of smaller companies that operate within global supply chains. The accessibility of these modern slavery statements is heavily dependent on civil society 'translating' the statements so that they are easily understood and readily digestible for the consumer. This requires a well-resourced civil society sector that has the time, funds and communication skills to make this information readily available to the general public.

Finally, the enforcement of both the Californian and UK laws is essentially outsourced to the market as neither law incorporates a holistic compliance framework that provides government with a central role in enforcing the law. Such a framework might include express penalties (in the form of fines or civil or criminal liability for non-compliance) to ensure the law is enforced, but it is broader than the issue of penalties. It should also require the government to publish a list of all organisations required to report under the law and ensure there is sufficient resourcing provided by governments to evaluate the statements and engage and educate business about modern slavery. Not only is no-one checking if companies are actually reporting, there are few consequences for not complying with the laws. An independent review of the UK *Modern Slavery Act* in

2018 recommended establishing a more ambitious enforcement model. The review suggested four stages of government enforcement for non-compliance: 'initial warnings, fines (as a percentage of turnover), court summons, and director disqualification'.[33] These recommendations, if implemented, would engender stronger compliance with the law.

In 2018, Australia passed its own modern slavery law. The Australian *Modern Slavery Act* applies to entities (including companies, not-for-profit organisations, universities and the Australian Government) based or operating in Australia, with an annual consolidated revenue of at least AU$100 million. These businesses are required to publish annual public statements (approved by the board) detailing the modern slavery risks in their operations and supply chains and the action they have taken to assess and address those risks, and the effectiveness of their response. The Australian *Modern Slavery Act* will capture an estimated 3000 business entities and it is the first modern slavery disclosure law in the world to impose reporting obligations on a national government and its agencies. The Act improves on the UK Act in that it includes mandatory reporting criteria and a central government repository to allow the modern slavery statements to be publicly accessible. Unfortunately, like the UK and Californian Acts, it does not include any real mechanisms for enforcing the law and does not include penalties (financial or otherwise) or incentives to induce compliance. Interestingly, like some of its counterparts in the UK, in its submission to the Australian Senate Inquiry into the establishment of the law, Nestlé Australia argued for stronger compliance provisions and noted that 'the absence of penalties will be counterproductive in the medium term, and that penalties for failure to report should be a focus of the three-year review'.[34]

In addition, Australia's most populous state, NSW, adopted a state-level Modern Slavery Act in June 2018, which applies to commercial organisations with NSW employees that supply goods or services for profit and have an annual turnover above AU$50 million. The NSW Act requires reporting entities to file an annual modern slavery statement and has broadly equivalent provisions to the UK and federal Australian Acts, with the significant and critical exception that it includes financial penalties (up to AU$1.1 million) for failure to meet the reporting requirements. The NSW Act will be complementary to the federal law and will focus on those companies that meet the reporting criteria and whose annual turnover is AU$50–100 million. The NSW *Modern Slavery Act* was introduced as a private member's bill and quickly passed through the state parliament. There was no assessment undertaken during the drafting process to forecast how many companies would be affected and how the government would effectively monitor compliance and issue penalties for non-compliance. The NSW *Modern Slavery Act* also establishes an Anti-Slavery Commissioner.

The Australian *Modern Slavery Act*, by contrast, was subject to extensive public consultation processes conducted over a period of nearly two years. These consultations commenced in February 2017, when a joint parliamentary inquiry into whether Australia should adopt national legislation to combat modern slavery was announced. Following lengthy public consultation, the Joint Parliamentary Inquiry Committee produced its final report in December 2017 and the Senate Legal and Constitutional Affairs Legislation Committee in 2018.[35] This period of consultation allowed business to get on board with the idea and as public awareness of the issue increased, it became reputationally risky for companies to publicly oppose it. In their submission to the Senate inquiry, Woolworths (one of the dominant supermarket chains in Australia) supported the introduction of an 'appropriately drafted Modern Slavery Act' and noted that '[f]or large, consumer-facing businesses such as Woolworths, our brand is our most important asset, and brand management is a critical aspect of the way our organisation operates'.[36] The campaign to establish a new modern slavery law was championed by a prominent Australian businessman and philanthropist, Andrew Forrest (of Fortescue Metals Group), and his public support for the law was no doubt helpful in garnering government attention and action.[37] The Forrest family also established the global anti-slavery organisation, Walk Free, which produces the Global Slavery Index. Even those who were not on board with the introduction of the new law found it difficult to oppose it outright. The NSW Farmers Association argued that '[w]hile we do not oppose the concept of a "Modern Slavery Act" in Australia, NSW Farmers believes existing legislation is already sufficient to protect against slave-like practices, particularly in the agriculture sector'.[38] The NSW Farmers Association have repeatedly argued against legislation such as the modern slavery laws, because they refuse to accept responsibility for transnational supply chains.

Ultimately, as succinctly stated by the Australian Government, 'there is no silver bullet to end modern slavery. Government, business, and civil society all have a role to play, and we need to work collaboratively'.[39] What remains unclear is that if there is no clear path to enforcing the law, are we also all responsible for a lack of results?

Transparency laws that go beyond modern slavery

Beyond the UK, Californian and Australian laws, which specifically target modern slavery practices in supply chains, there has been a slow trickle of laws emerging in other countries that have put corporations on notice that they need to be more transparent about their sourcing strategies. Each of these laws mandates differing levels of corporate social disclosure and proposes a variety of compliance mechanisms to achieve this.

The 2017 French Duty of Vigilance Law[40] stands apart from the Californian, UK and Australian laws as it is broader in scope (in that it targets potential effects by companies on all human rights in supply chains, not just modern slavery practices) and incorporates more concrete compliance mechanisms. It also differs significantly because it utilises human rights due diligence (or vigilance) as a key mechanism for improving respect for human rights in supply chains. The French law establishes a duty of vigilance in the French Commercial Code; that is, a legal obligation of prudent and diligent conduct, owed by the parent companies of groups that employ at least 5000 employees in France or 10 000 employees worldwide. The duty of vigilance consists of establishing, effectively implementing and publishing 'reasonable vigilance measures adequate to identify risks and to prevent severe impacts on human rights and fundamental freedoms, on the health and safety of individuals and on the environment' (article 1). The law sets out the parameters of what is meant by vigilance, but it broadly refers to the process of identifying and addressing the human rights impacts of a business across its operations, products and supply chains. This vigilance should include assessments of internal procedures and systems, as well as external engagement with groups potentially affected by its operations. The French law provides for stronger enforcement measures than the Australian, UK and Californian modern slavery laws: a court may impose an injunction on companies to comply with the vigilance requirements and companies may potentially be held liable under a civil lawsuit (not criminally liable) where companies have failed to implement due diligence plans and harm has occurred. Critically, compliance here is not linked simply to a failure to report, but a failure to implement. The French law applies to France's largest companies (as determined by the number of employees), estimated to be approximately 200–300 businesses. The first corporate vigilance plans were released in 2018, and a French activist organisation, Sherpa, noted that the reports were 'particularly short, [and] are of a lightness that contrasts with the importance of the stakes of the Law on the Duty of Vigilance'.[41] Their assessment noted that one company operating in the extractives sectors released a short six-page plan, which covered its more than 900 subsidiaries operating in nearly 130 countries.

In May 2019, the Netherlands adopted the Child Labour Due Diligence Law that will require all companies selling products in the Netherlands to submit a statement to the regulatory authorities declaring that they have carried out due diligence to address the risks of child labour in their global supply chains.[42] Many Dutch businesses opposed this law (and suggested a continuation of voluntary efforts would be sufficient) but a group of over 40 Dutch companies, led by chocolate maker Tony's Chocolonely, and including several high-profile companies like Heineken and ABN AMRO, supported the law. Since 2014, the Dutch

Government has been encouraging certain Dutch business sectors most at risk of having a negative effect on human rights to negotiate responsible business conduct agreements with Dutch civil society, trade unions and government. Several agreements have so far been established, including in the garment and textiles sector and the banking sector[43] and others in gold, forestry, food and insurance sectors are in different stages of development. Socialising the idea of due diligence through these sector-specific agreements was a useful precursor to establishing the 2019 law.

There are several relevant US laws that target corporate sourcing practices in supply chains. In 2010, the UN Joint Human Rights Office in the Democratic Republic of the Congo (DRC) reported that more than 300 civilians were raped by armed groups in three villages located close to mining sites in North Kivu province. The UN investigation revealed a link between the violence and competition over access to so-called conflict minerals (gold, tin, tungsten and tantalum), some of which are commonly used in the production of electronic goods, such as phones and computers.[44] Partly in response to this, the US adopted section 1502 of the *Dodd-Frank Act 2010*,[45] which creates a reporting requirement for publicly traded companies in the US with products containing these conflict minerals. The reporting requirements in the law were an attempt to expose and stem the trade in conflict minerals and thus reduce the human rights abuses. Like the UK, Californian and

Australian laws, this US law does not place a ban or penalty on the activity itself (the *use* of conflict minerals), but rather aims to make it more transparent. If companies discover they have been sourcing conflict minerals from the DRC or adjoining countries, it is not illegal for them to continue doing so; however, they must report this to the US Securities Exchange Commission. Functionally, it relies on the adverse reputational impact of such a disclosure rather than mandating penalties for actually sourcing minerals from conflict-afflicted regions. While section 1502 does not impose penalties for not reporting or complying in good faith, the information filed by companies is subject to section 18 of the *Securities Exchange Act 1934*, which attaches liability for any false or misleading statements. Initial analysis of the various statements submitted under these laws indicate that, to date, like the corporate responses to the modern slavery laws, the disclosures tend to be more symbolic than substantive. For example, in a study analysing the first statements issued under section 1502 of the *Dodd-Frank Act*, the reports indicated a low level of compliance with the requirements of the law[46] and many companies failed to follow the basic procedural requirements of the transparency provision. The European Union has also adopted a similar law targeting conflict minerals, which will be effective from 2021 (*Conflict Minerals Regulation 2021* (EU)).

The US also has the *Tariff Act of 1930* (s 307 amended in 2016), which applies to all US importers and allows the government to apply a temporary withholding or conclusive ban of goods that are suspected to be the result of forced labour, and the Federal Acquisitions Regulations (subpart 22.17 amended in 2015), which requires qualifying government contractors and subcontractors to certify that they have made efforts to ensure their supply chain is free from forced labour and human trafficking. Failure to comply may result in a termination of the procurement contract. The US Department of Labor issues a list of products it believes are produced by forced labour, which includes some very broad categories such as bamboo from Myanmar, bricks from China and India, carpets from Nepal and Pakistan, cocoa and coffee from Côte d'Ivoire, cotton from China and Uzbekistan, clothing from Vietnam, rubber from Thailand and toys from China. In February 2019, the US issued a detention order on Taiwanese-imported seafood from a fishing vessel (Tunago No. 61) that Greenpeace had exposed as using forced labour. Greenpeace documented working conditions that included the crew working 20-hour days, seven days a week, and facing physical violence, verbal abuse and a lack of food and water.[47] Since 2004, Brazil has published a 'dirty list' disclosing companies that have engaged in illicit labour practices, who are then banned from accessing any public financing.[48]

In addition, there are several laws in progress around the world that aim to expose corporate human rights abuses in global supply chains. Switzerland is debating a law (the Responsible Business Initiative) that would require companies to conduct mandatory due diligence on their human rights impacts and be legally liable for the activities of their subsidiaries. Hong Kong, Canada and the US have proposed new thematic laws focused exclusively on modern slavery. The Hong Kong draft Modern Slavery Bill was introduced in 2017 and is based on the UK Act. A Modern Slavery Bill was tabled in the Canadian House of Commons in December 2018; it would require companies to publicly release a report every year, detailing what they have done to ensure their supply chains are transparent and free of goods and materials fully or partially produced by child or forced labour. The bill would also give the Canadian Border Service Agency the power to ban these products and impose fines up to C$250 000. In October 2018, the *Business Supply Chain Transparency on Trafficking and Slavery Act of 2018* (H.R. 7089) was put before the US House of Representatives for consideration. The law would require certain companies to disclose information describing any measures the company has taken to identify and address conditions of forced labour, slavery, human trafficking, and the worst forms of child labour within the company's supply chains. The annual report would be posted on the company's website and the website of the Securities Exchange Commission.

Important but imperfect laws

What these new laws aim to do is shine a spotlight on modern slavery in supply chains. Shining a light on abusive practices is a useful step towards addressing the problem. In the wise words of Louis Brandeis (former US Supreme Court justice), 'publicity is justly commended as a remedy for social and industrial diseases. Sunlight is said to be the best of disinfectants'.[49] Consecutive modern slavery laws have introduced key improvements and, on balance, are steps in the right direction. However, these modern slavery laws don't force companies to change their practices or remedy the problems they find. The French and Dutch vigilance laws stand apart from other laws with their focus on prevention, not just reporting. Institutionalising transparency will not automatically reduce modern slavery in corporate supply chains, but increased transparency is a useful first step along the road to reform. The establishment of an independent Anti-Slavery Commissioner in both the UK and in the NSW state law is useful in raising awareness and educating companies and the public about the need for these laws. The Australian federal Act did not include provision for this role and this may be something the government should reconsider upon its three-year review of the law. Whether such a commissioner should also have enforcement powers is a question open for debate.

The Australian and UK modern slavery reporting regimes both require the publication of annual statements.

The benefits of this approach are threefold. It facilitates the dissemination of knowledge about corporate best practice in addressing modern slavery, (potentially) exposes laggards and, assuming the reports are consistent over time, enables company measures to be assessed longitudinally. The most recent Australian laws have built upon the earlier legal disclosure models and enacted modern slavery legislation with key refinements – namely, government-operated public registers, financial penalties (NSW only), mandatory reporting against specified criteria and public procurement provisions. Modern slavery legislation is, at the very least, generating a broader understanding of the risks associated with consumptive spending and supply chain sourcing. What is not clear is whether they are sufficient to fix the problem.

There are several outstanding questions around the efficacy of the current disclosure models and whether such laws can result in a substantive improvement in working conditions in global supply chains. Critically, none of them is a holistic approach to compliance that includes resourcing a government department to monitor compliance and penalties for non-compliance, thus hampering accountability. Consequently, under the UK Act, non-reporting is widespread, with fewer than a half of businesses required to publish a statement reportedly having done so.[50] The standard of disclosures is low, with minimum requirements failing to be met. It is too early to determine whether this experience will be repeated in Australia. A UK activist group, Focus on Labour Exploitation (FLEX), argues that the transparency requirement of the *Modern Slavery Act* needs to be recognised for what it is: a soft requirement that requires businesses to take no specific actions against slavery, and only to report on what, if anything, they are doing.

The core dilemma of regulation is when to punish and when to persuade.[51] Fines and sanctions are, of course, not the only way to regulate misconduct, but the business and human rights agenda has been labouring under reliance on the self-regulatory corporate 'self-enlightenment' model for some time. Waiting for companies to uniformly and consistently regulate themselves to prevent human rights abuses is akin to waiting for Godot. Based on the past few decades, where there have been sufficient examples of corporate irresponsibility to shake our belief in the value of the self-regulatory model, reliance on this method seems like naively asking the fox to guard the hen house. When left to depend primarily on ethics or market pressure for enforcement, compliance will likely be reduced to the bare minimum.

Even with refinements, modern slavery reporting regimes are inherently limited, requiring companies to report, rather than to act, and attaching only indirect liability for human right abuses through shortcomings in reporting. The assumption that greater transparency and availability of information about companies' activities will translate into improvements in practice and increased corporate accountability remains largely untested. While modern slavery disclosures may reveal that companies are adopting, or refining, policies and practices aimed at addressing modern slavery, it remains to be seen whether this actually changes corporate behaviour and results in greater respect for workers' rights on the factory floor. Nor is it yet clear whether these laws will result in greater corporate legal accountability for inaction in addressing modern slavery. One lesson from the review of misconduct in Australia's banking sector may be pertinent here. In contemplating the lack of accountability for misconduct in Australia's financial sector, a 2019 report notes that 'misconduct will be deterred only if entities believe that misconduct will be detected, denounced and justly punished'.[52] Misconduct is unlikely to be deterred if it relies solely on consumers becoming aware of the problem and responding by reducing their purchases or custom from the relevant companies.

An essential element of what companies should be reporting on is their due diligence efforts to prevent and redress incidences of modern slavery, something the broader French law institutionalises. Reporting is simply the final step in the process of identifying, assessing and addressing modern slavery risks, and tracking the effectiveness of those responses. For reporting to be both useful and legitimate, it should be based on effective human rights due diligence that has both a preventative and remedial framework.

WHAT IS HUMAN RIGHTS DUE DILIGENCE?

The UN Guiding Principles on Business and Human Rights provide a broad framework that sets out the general parameters of what companies should consider when conducting human rights due diligence assessments. Namely, businesses are expected to:

1. assess their actual and potential adverse human rights impacts
2. integrate these findings internally and take appropriate preventative and mitigating action
3. track the effectiveness of their response
4. publicly communicate how they are addressing their human rights impacts.

A key feature that distinguishes human rights due diligence from traditional corporate due diligence (which might be used, for example, when a company is acquiring another company) is that human rights due diligence focuses primarily on detecting the risks that the company may impose on others, as opposed to risks to the company itself. As such, human rights due diligence is designed to be an ongoing, interactive mechanism that keeps the company apprised of its impact on workers, the community and a broader set of stakeholders. In applying human rights due diligence to address modern slavery risks, it is also useful to apply a 'gender lens'. Women are disproportionately affected by modern slavery, as they are made more vulnerable by patriarchal norms and discriminatory economic structures. It is estimated that women and girls account for 71 per cent of the estimated global number of the more than 40 million people trapped in slavery.[53] One expert argues:

> businesses should conduct gender-sensitive human rights due diligence to find out the nature and extent of slavery in their supply chains. Collaboration and consultation with women's organisations should help businesses in identifying hidden forms of slavery. They should also collect and disclose gender disaggregated data in their annual reports as well as in tracking progress in eradicating contemporary forms of slavery.[54]

The current laws are focused on getting companies to report on their commitments to tackle these problems, rather than assessing their performance and incorporating a remedy to directly redress the harm. Reporting must measure outcomes, not just process. It is essential to ensure that the laws encourage substantive compliance with human rights standards, rather than merely symbolic compliance. Substantive compliance must encompass tangible actions to satisfy the true objective of the law. For example, what practical steps are companies taking to prevent and reduce modern slavery practices in supply chains, what problems are they finding and what are they doing to address them. Ticking boxes will not stop modern slavery.

Leveraging change

In 1954, when the US Supreme Court ruled that racial segregation of children in public schools was unconstitutional in the landmark case of *Brown v. Board of Education*, it was regarded as game changer for the civil rights movement. Passage of the *Civil Rights Act of 1964* followed, then the *Voting Rights Act of 1965* and the *Fair Housing Act of 1968* in an ongoing effort to stamp out endemic racial discrimination. Each of these laws was a significant lever that influenced subsequent social and legal changes in the US, but law by itself is likely to be insufficient to ensure sustained cultural change. In 2016, the US Government Accountability Office released a report showing the percentage of all K–12 public schools that had high proportions of poor and black or Hispanic students increased from 9 to 16 per cent. Moreover, these schools were incredibly racially and economically concentrated: 75 to 100 per cent of the students were black or Hispanic and poor.[55] Sixty years after *Brown v. Board of Education*, many US classrooms remain segregated. In 2013, the US witnessed the emergence of the 'black lives matter' movement in an effort to intervene and disrupt a society that was perceived as still 'systematically and intentionally' targeting black people in the US.[56] As happened during the 1950s and 1960s in the US, laws can stimulate social change or solidify and legitimise change that has already occurred, but reliance on law alone will not create sustained social change without broader support from other stakeholders including individuals, communities and businesses. Modern slavery laws are one (important) piece of the puzzle in better protecting workers in supply chains, but alongside legal reforms, government, business and society more generally have broader roles to play.

In the aftermath of the Rana Plaza factory collapse in Bangladesh in 2013 that killed more than 1100 workers, it was revealed that Bangladesh had fewer than 200 government inspectors carrying out factory labour inspections of more than 5000 factories with more than four million workers.[57] This problem is not isolated to the developing world. FLEX notes that the UK currently, 'has an under-staffed labour inspectorate, less than half the global benchmark of one inspector per 10 000 workers'.[58] UK employers can expect a minimum wage inspection on average once every 500 years. Given this minimal scrutiny of labour conditions in the UK, it should come as no surprise that modern slavery can be found both within and beyond its borders in many UK supply chains. This lapse in government enforcement places a greater burden of responsibility on businesses and worker representatives to ensure safe working conditions. Beyond passing new laws, government must also be committed to ensuring they are implemented and, like in Australia under the new *Modern Slavery Act*, lead by example to make its own supply chains more transparent.

As governments have more purchasing power than many companies combined, there are several ways in which public spending can be used to protect labour and human rights. Governments could adopt and enforce strict ethical procurement policies and demand decent working conditions as a prerequisite to obtaining a government contract; for example, they could insist on limits to subcontracting and the use of flexible labour. To determine the exposure to potential exploitation in their supply chains, governments could also perform due diligence that identifies the risk of abuses on the basis of geography, industry and type of commodity that they source. Governments could furthermore impose requirements on companies that compete for tenders or organisations that receive funding. For example, any prospective government supplier could be asked to conduct human rights due diligence in line with international standards, to have visibility over certain parts of their supply chain, or to be able to demonstrate the chain of custody of certain commodities. In addition, they could be asked to demonstrate what actions they are taking to prevent or mitigate the risk of labour and human rights abuses. Such measures would send a clear message to current and prospective suppliers, as compliance would be a necessity to engage in any financial transaction with the government, while non-compliance would result in the termination of contracts and exclusion from future lucrative government tenders.

Alongside government, business must also play its role and make a meaningful commitment to human rights as part of business as usual, not the exception. The independent review of the UK *Modern Slavery Act* argued, 'companies need to feel an equal pressure to report slavery as they do on equality. Failure to comply with modern slavery obligations should be viewed on the same level as failure to file accurate accounts or prevent bribery and corruption'.[59] The UK has had an Equal Pay Act since 1970, but disparities remain between what is paid to men and women for doing the same job. New regulations introduced in 2017 now require UK employers with more than 250 employees to disclose their data on the gender pay gap, and they may be fined for not doing so (however, like the UK *Modern Slavery*

Act, initial enforcement is relying on transparency to encourage compliance). Ensuring substantive compliance with the law means that there must be a robust and systematic approach in place to deal with non-compliance, and business must also integrate human rights concerns into its mainstream business operations. In 2018, the US State Department reported that, compared to the nearly 25 million people estimated to be working as modern-day slaves, there were only 7045 convictions reported globally for human-trafficking offences and of these only 332 related to forced labour-trafficking cases.[60]

Compliance with the law is just one driver in the efforts to develop more responsible supply chains. Other important factors include addressing the business model (creating more efficient yet sustainable supply chains), leveraging reputation (responding to consumer, investor or civil society expectations) and utilising organisational changes (including top to bottom commitments to human rights, broader external collaboration and a focus on worker empowerment).

The basic business model, specifically, the purchasing practices of buyers at the top of the supply chain (often, but not always, brand-focused companies), has a significant impact on the conditions faced by workers at the bottom. Yet while these lead companies have shown a readiness to impose occasional requirements on their suppliers through demands to open their factories, fields and mines to social auditors, the companies at the top of the chain have shown limited willingness, to date, to holistically address the effects of their own practices and innovate in the way in which they do business. One of the limitations of the new modern slavery disclosure laws (and CSR programs more generally) is that, although well meaning, 'they are aimed at treating the symptoms of the problem rather than tackling the underlying causes: the very nature of the business model'.[61] Arguably, this is partly due to the broader competitive environment within which businesses operate. Companies are subject to a range of market and financial pressures, which are in turn passed down the chain to suppliers, which exert systemic downward pressure on workers' rights. Short-term profit expectations of shareholders combined with pricing pressure from consumers propel the ongoing search for lower costs of production.[62]

However, the good news is that a 2019 Bain & Company survey found that 90 per cent of company representatives believe they need to change their core business model, at least partly, in order to operate in a truly sustainable economy, and 38 per cent believe their core business model will need to change radically.[63] Too many CSR or sustainability departments within large companies are siloed from their procurement colleagues, and decisions about where and when to purchase goods and services are isolated from human rights concerns. Companies that are committed to mitigating modern slavery risks in their supply chains need to assess their own purchasing practices as a source of risk. Companies need to look both outward and inward when pressing for reforms. Some companies have started to move from a transactional sourcing model, with fixed terms and conditions for suppliers, to a model based on a longer-term relationship with suppliers, in which some terms can be re-negotiated.[64] What is needed is for all companies, large and small, to come to the table, and factor compliance and human rights due diligence into their own practices and business models, including adjusting their pricing structure and lead times for orders. A 2017 report by the International Labour Organization (ILO) found that buyers impose 'extreme pressure on suppliers' price quotes'.[65] The ILO study reported that 39 per cent of suppliers surveyed accepted orders 'whose price did not allow them to cover production costs'.[66] Innovative and responsible supply chain management requires companies to view the world as it is not and consider what it might be, rather than continue to adopt incremental changes to how it is.

Reputational risk is often referred to as a driver towards developing more sustainable practices that integrate concern for human rights into the business model, but the jury is still out on how effective that is.[67] This is a critical issue, because the current modern slavery laws largely depend on external pressures to motivate companies to comply. Over the past 40 years, companies such as Nike, Shell, Nestlé, Apple, BHP, Monsanto, Walmart, Kmart, Microsoft, Disney, Chevron and Exxon are just a few of those who have been called to publicly account for their corporate irresponsibility. Still, these companies and others like them 'remain dominant players and their profits are sky high'.[68] However, there is a flip side to 'naming and shaming' and that is 'naming and faming'. Companies that have made concerted improvements in their modern slavery statements, such as Marks & Spencer in the UK, have been widely praised both for their efforts and the improvement of the detail provided in their reports over time.

The power of consumers is potentially a critical tool in influencing business behaviour in relation to modern slavery, but it will be most effective for consumer-facing companies whose reputation is critical in maintaining goodwill with consumers. While there is now increasing (if still limited) information available for diligent consumers to develop more awareness about how and where the goods they buy are produced, there is more work to be done in synthesising this information and amplifying the voice of the consumer. While it is an admirable goal to leverage purchasing power to eradicate modern slavery in supply chains, this will be most effective when done in combination with other levers that can drive change in corporate practices.

One of these levers is the reliance on companies for investment. Investors can play a critical role in influencing corporate behaviour. Investors, whether they be banks, pension funds, mutual funds or insurance companies, have a proactive part to play in reducing

MARKS & SPENCER: TRACKING THE REPORTS

Over time the modern slavery statements from UK retailer Marks & Spencer have evolved to now more comprehensively identifying the real risks of modern slavery in its supply chains and the actions it is taking to address them.

2015/16: M&S describes relevant policies and its Global Sourcing Principles, but provides little information about identified risks.

2016/17: M&S expounds on its policies, governance structure and strategy for addressing modern slavery; describes its engagement with civil society groups and affected stakeholders; and identifies numerous examples of product-based and geographical risks of modern slavery in its supply chain that it plans to continue to monitor.

2017/18: M&S details new initiatives with expert civil society organisations to conduct human rights impact assessments, the process through which it identifies the impacts, and the outcomes of the assessment, including a description of the risks identified through case studies and the changes in company practice as a result of the assessment.[69]

modern slavery risk. Investors can and should be asking companies to do more: to audit their supply chains, to provide full transparency over where materials are coming from, who is making them and the conditions in which those workers are operating. Adequate disclosure may also enable more informed conversations between investors and their investees and contribute to investors fulfilling their own responsibility to respect human rights. But when investors are asked if it is 'important to consider human rights in investment decision-making … some will tell you that, while human rights are important, it is not always possible or even permissible to consider them in practice'.[70] However, some investors are actively pushing companies to embrace a purpose beyond profit maximisation.

In early 2019, Larry Fink, CEO of BlackRock, the world's largest investor with US$6 trillion under management, announced that 'his company would change its hiring and potentially its compensation structure to advance diversity and ensure that five years from now the company is not just "a bunch of white men"'.[71] Some critics, harking back to the days of Milton Friedman, suggested that 'this is fundamentally not the role of a public company and it's unfair to investors who may not agree with his politics'.[72] However, arguably the pendulum is swinging towards rather than away from Fink's approach and embracing a greater acceptance of responsibility by investors to incorporate human rights in their investment decisions. As of 2017, 78 per cent of the world's 250 largest companies disclosed non-financial data in their annual financial reports.[73] In a 2019 briefing paper, Shift, an organisation that advises business about human rights, argued that investors have a critical role to play in tackling risks, like modern slavery, that are present deep in company supply chains. Shift acknowledges that the 'financial sector has generally been slower than other sectors to embrace this responsibility'.[74]

Finally, companies must look both inward and outward to consider what organisational changes they need to make to reduce the risk of modern slavery and more broadly embrace human rights in their business operations. Both the UK and Australian modern slavery laws require a company's board to sign off on its modern slavery statement, which is a useful and necessary requirement towards encouraging greater vertical integration of human rights concerns within the company. Companies should also look outward to engage a broad range of stakeholders, including their workers, in creating more responsible supply chains. Many supply chain workers are isolated and not formally organised within trade unions, and don't have access to advice or legal assistance. New and emerging technologies that provide workers with greater access to information enable them to share their experiences and collectively advocate for better conditions, which may assist in improving their plight.[75] Like law, technology alone cannot fix structural inequalities, missing institutional capacity, or a lack of political will to address labour exploitation. But when used responsibly and with worker protection and outcomes as a priority, it offers an opportunity for companies to engage with and address worker concerns.

Worker-organising campaigns, particularly those targeting consumer-facing companies, such as the multi-year Fair Food campaign initiated by the Coalition of Imokalee Workers (CIW) in the US, also illustrate the potential of organised workers and civil society organisations to affect business practices. The CIW is a membership-based human rights organisation of farm workers that emerged to address the abusive recruitment and working conditions facing tomato pickers (predominantly migrant workers) in Florida. The campaign, driven by farm workers themselves, relied on strong alliance building with consumer groups and human rights activists to persuade major brands to take steps to end farm-worker exploitation. Through an initial boycott of the fast-food company Taco Bell, publicity campaigns and protests, the campaign was ultimately successful in gaining the participation of several large companies, including McDonalds, Sodexo, Subway, Whole Foods, Burger King and Walmart, in its Fair Food Code of Conduct.[76] The Food Code addresses modern slavery risks, including recruitment abuses, by prohibiting labour intermediaries and mandating that growers hire all field workers directly.[77] The Food Code is backed by binding agreements between the CIW and the buyer companies, which obligate the buyers to suspend purchases from growers who have failed to comply with the

Food Code. This places a strong market incentive on growers to comply with the Food Code. When workers know their rights and are able to organise, they also act to prevent modern slavery, which is entirely consistent with the declared objectives of governments and businesses who have expressed adherence to new laws to tackle modern slavery.

Ultimately, if the new modern slavery laws are to work, governments need to enforce them, companies must incorporate human rights into their business-as-usual supply chain operations, consumers and investors should use their leverage and collaborate with others to increase their influence, and workers must be empowered to have a seat at the table in addressing the problem. What this means is that all of these players must focus not on the risks to business from uncovering modern slavery in their supply chain, but on the real and tangible risks to workers of becoming modern-day slaves and how to prevent and redress those risks.

5

Frontiers in the fight against modern slavery

The dark side of innovation is key to making modern slavery into a 'business success'. Exploiters continue to find novel ways to take advantage of people's misfortune. They see opportunities in other people's despair and manage to profit through new-found forms of illegal control. Fortunately, innovation is also occurring on the frontlines in the fight against modern slavery. There are progressive discussions about the role of the state and the responsibilities of business; continuing activities by non-governmental organisations (NGOs) and trade unions; a rising interest in ethical consumption; and technological advances such as the use of big data, artificial intelligence and blockchain. While the use of disruptive technology can often boggle the mind, other novel approaches are low-tech and simply arise from having a better understanding of the dynamics around modern slavery.

These developments can help to avoid and remediate forced labour and exploitation, but it is important to caution that there is no quick fix for modern slavery. It is unlikely that any innovative practice will make a big difference in isolation. The proliferation of modern slavery should be explained in the context of broader developments such as economic globalisation, the international fragmentation of production, the changing nature of work, migration trends and growing inequality. By themselves, none of these factors explains the existence and rise of forced labour. Yet together, they paint a much clearer picture. Similarly, strategies to combat modern slavery should always be holistic. There is no magic bullet to end modern slavery. If we make the mistake of looking for a single cure and neglect to confront modern slavery on multiple fronts, we end up treating the symptoms of human trafficking and forced labour rather than dealing with its root causes.

Reaffirming the role of the state

It is debatable whether the state (that is, government) has the ability and willingness to play a bigger – and more effective – role in the fight against modern slavery. However, since the United Nations (UN) has formulated the goal to end human trafficking and modern slavery by 2030, maintaining the status quo is simply not an option. The neoliberal policy agenda has seen governments around the world largely withdraw from regulating (global) business matters. The subsequent regime of voluntarism and self-regulation of social matters by companies has failed to deliver change. The labour and human rights abuses detailed in previous chapters illustrate that private governance alone is a poor substitute for public governance. Fortunately, whether we should rely on strong state intervention or unrestrained free markets is not a zero-sum proposition. The deceptively simple question is how much we need of each in order to get the best outcome for society. This is not merely about the degree of state intervention; it is also about the type of state intervention.

For example, governments have traditionally approached modern slavery and trafficking as criminal matters, to be tackled through the criminal justice system. Unfortunately, considering the large number of people in modern slavery conditions around the world, there have been very few prosecutions. In 2016, only 1038 people were convicted worldwide for forced labour and human trafficking.[1] In 2018 in the UK, 239 suspects were charged and 185 were found guilty of modern slavery offences. While legislation in the US requires convicted traffickers to pay victims the amount that was earned from them, judges ordered perpetrators to pay in only 27 per cent of cases between

2013 and 2016. During the previous three-year period, payment was ordered in 36 per cent of the cases.[2] Similarly, while a 2016 law in the US bans slave-made imports, as of 2019 the value of seized shipments amounted to only US$6.3 million, 0.0015 per cent of the US$400 billion in goods tainted by modern slavery believed to enter the country each year.[3]

There is no doubt that modern slavery is illegal. However, even if the number of prosecutions were to increase, or if the amount of restitution paid to victims were to go up and more slave-made goods seized, these efforts only provide solace after forced labour and other abuses have already taken place. By regarding modern slavery predominantly as a criminal matter, the state is taking a reactive approach. By not approaching modern slavery as a broader and more complex human rights and labour issue, it is neglecting to proactively address the underlying causes.

Yet there are some signs that suggest an increasingly active role of the state. Previous chapters have outlined developments in some places, including the UK and Australia, in which the state has proactively legislated in an attempt to make companies address modern slavery. However, the introduced modern slavery laws mainly require companies to publicly disclose their efforts to address modern slavery. It leaves companies free to decide what kinds of steps to take, there are few consequences for non-compliance, and the laws do not incorporate any requirement to remedy the problem. It is therefore questionable whether simply introducing reporting requirements will effectuate sustained and substantive change.

A parallel can be drawn with the position of women in the corporate world. Laws that mandate corporate reporting on gender equality have existed in many countries for years, yet women are still drastically under-represented in senior positions. Conversely, in Norway, mandatory quotas for women on corporate boards and the threat of large fines has seen half of board seats swiftly being filled by women. This implies that it is likely to be more effective for the state to be prescriptive and to penalise companies that do not comply with legislation, rather than only asking companies to disclose information about a certain issue.

Governments could, therefore, build on current modern slavery laws by being more prescriptive about the manner in which companies need to avoid and remediate forced labour. A good starting point is to align legislation with the UN Guiding Principles on Business and Human Rights (UN Guiding Principles) and due diligence guides such as those produced by the Organisation for Economic Co-operation and Development (OECD). The due diligence process is the key to transforming the UN Guiding Principles from principles to practice. Due diligence refers to the practice of identifying and addressing a company's human rights impact across operations and in supplier networks. Since the publication of the UN Guiding Principles in 2011, there have been significant advances in further defining and refining the concept.

The OECD has been particularly active in this space and has released updated sector-specific guidelines for conducting due diligence for supply chains in the conflict minerals, garment and footwear, agricultural and financial sectors.[4] Yet, while this kind of due diligence is increasingly mentioned in corporate policies and reports, there is often little clarity as to what this actually entails and what specific action the company has undertaken to identify modern slavery risks. For a company to reliably *know and show* that it is not violating human rights and for that information to be consistent among companies within a specific sector, the state should be more prescriptive about due diligence requirements, while including sanctions for non-compliance (such as in France and the Netherlands). However, even where the law is clear, enforcement is the key. This requires adequate government resources to both monitor non-compliance and the political will to follow through with sanctions when required.

Another key element of the UN Guiding Principles is the need for both governments and companies to provide victims with access to remedies for human rights abuses. This may include providing access to judicial (for example, court action) and non-judicial (remedies available outside of the courts) mechanisms. Survivors of modern slavery face significant barriers to accessing remedies. This includes cost, time, lack of legal advice, and limited knowledge of existing ways to seek redress. Through legislation, governments could facilitate better access to remedy. They could, for example, amend the evidentiary record requirements that workers must produce to prove wage underpayment, provide access to government workplace advice helplines, impose a legal requirement on companies to advise workers about available grievance mechanisms to hear and settle complaints, place the onus on the employer rather than the worker to prove a violation did not occur, and enable greater transparency around some workplace records.

For example, in Australia, the New South Wales (NSW) Mandatory Retailer Code applies to all retailers and suppliers, wherever they are based, who sell clothing products within NSW that have been manufactured or altered in Australia. The code requires the inclusion of mandatory terms in contracts, which require contractors and subcontractors in the supply chain to inform them where and under what conditions goods are produced, including, on request, disclosing such information to the state enforcement agency and the trade union. The recovery mechanism is also innovative in that it reverses the traditional onus of proof, so that unless the relevant company can prove that a claimant worker has not done the work or that the claim calculation is erroneous, the company will be obliged to pay the claimed wages within a specified time.

Regardless of the (modern slavery) laws and amendments that are introduced, it is vital that governments

BRAZIL'S DIRTY LIST

In Brazil, the government has dedicated significant resources to increasing its labour inspection teams. It is estimated that since 1995, 45 000 workers have been freed from slavery.[5] In addition, a multi-stakeholder group (including the International Labour Organization and several NGOs) established a National Pact for the Eradication of Slave Labour whereby companies could voluntarily and publicly pledge to reduce modern slavery by 'cutting commercial ties with businesses that have made use of slave labour, incorporating contractual clauses ... implementing mechanisms to track products and provid[e] in-house training for employees and trading partners'.[6] In addition to such voluntary action, the Brazilian government, in 2004, launched a 'dirty list' (Ministry of Labour and Employment Decree No. 540/2004), which is a public register of companies found by governmental inspectors to have forced labour in their supply chains. Companies named on the list are monitored for two years and are also subject to fines. The 'dirty list' is reinforced by a further governmental decree (Decree No. 1 150), which recommends that financial bodies refrain from granting financial assistance to companies on the list. Persistent pushback and legal attacks from business interests resulted in a temporary suspension of the publication of the list, and the listing process has been revised to provide more legal guarantees for companies being assessed by the labour inspection teams. The Brazilian approach combines public and private regulatory mechanisms to reduce modern slavery and recognises that the government must make a significant resource commitment in order for such strategies to have a chance of success.

prepare for the potential flow-on effects. While the UK introduced the first national modern slavery law that mandates corporate reporting on this issue, the government has not provided sufficient support for victims, according to a report by the Winston Churchill Memorial Trust. Its author, a legal expert specialising in trafficking cases, said that 'the US and Europe both have models for long-term support for victims; however, the UK is lagging behind'.[7] The US allows victims to stay in the country for four years and offers a pathway to permanent residency. The UK usually only grants a one-year stay, while the path to remain in the country permanently is complicated. Conversely, while Belgium and the Netherlands don't have modern slavery legislation that require companies to report on this issue, both countries do grant victims free legal assistance, a privilege reserved for defendants in the UK, while providing victims with housing and counselling for a longer period of time.[8]

This lack of support in the UK occurs at a time where a record number of modern slavery victims are being referred to authorities. For instance, in 2018, 2118 child slaves were registered in the UK – an increase of two-thirds from 2016. However, a quarter of victims in the care of authorities went missing at least once, according to research by Every Child Protected Against Trafficking, with some feared to have returned to their traffickers after being treated like criminals or illegal immigrants by authorities.[9] Reasons for running away include poor accommodation, fear of authorities and the ongoing control of exploiters.[10] Conversely, after a successful pilot, 12 modern slavery survivors from countries including Brazil, Gambia and Sri Lanka participated in a 10-week course at Northern College in the UK in which they were taught computer skills and English. Northern College is in talks with the education ministry about further funding to extend this pilot.[11] This pilot found that, for survivors, access to education and work is as important as appropriate housing and counselling.

Proactive government action on modern slavery does not only mean implementing laws that directly target forced labour and human trafficking or dealing with the flow-on effects of such laws. If we regard modern slavery as a complex labour and human rights issue, and consider its causes, then a host of legislative options becomes apparent. For example, previous chapters detail the plight of brick-kiln workers in Cambodia and small-hold farmers in the Philippines. Respectively, their predicament is caused by the predatory microfinance industry and the buying of agricultural land under unfair conditions. In principle, while microfinance and land ownership can empower workers, the lack of state oversight in these cases has resulted in debt traps and unconscionable contracts. Lack of (access to) equitable finance is particularly acute for women, who make up 71 per cent of the global modern slavery population. For example, 'in Nigeria, a woman is 32% less likely than a man to own a formal bank account; in

Bangladesh it is 41% ... Migrant workers have limited options to ... carry out everyday life transactions'.[12] Governments can play a valuable role regulating the finance industry, including microfinance and ensuring equitable conditions in which farmers, women and migrant workers can better negotiate financial terms and transactions to help avoid and redress modern slavery. It can thus be effective for the state to more actively intervene in the market.

In the discussion of the supermarket supply chains in chapter 2, we saw that the cost pressures created by large companies at the top of supply chains can result in labour exploitation by suppliers. These market forces can be curbed if the state uses competition laws to intervene in cases where market concentration results in anti-competitive behaviour and the misuse of market power.[13] Another example of intervention in the market is the introduction of a minimum wage set at the level of a living wage in the country of production. Particularly if adopted in export-oriented countries, this will lift millions out of poverty and reduce the chance they will be caught in debt traps and forced labour.

For example, about 70 per cent of all hazelnuts come from Turkey. Production is marked by low wages, wage theft, and bonded and child labour.[14] Many of the seasonal hazelnut workers are vulnerable Syrian refugees. The minimum wage is insufficient to keep a family above the poverty line and recruiters who connect these workers with the jobs often take a cut from the workers' wages. As Turkey's Labour Code does not apply to farms with fewer than 50 employees, the state has effectively removed itself from policing this problem. Monitoring of working conditions and ensuring payment of wages is left to companies like Ferrero – a privately held company that is the third largest chocolate maker in the world – which refuses to disclose information about its supply chain.[15] The state could also intervene by setting minimum wages and/or prices for goods.

Ethiopia's emerging apparel industry shows that, while artificially low wages may be successful in attracting foreign firms, the result is that workers become trapped in a downward spiral. Ethiopia has recently sought to insert itself into global garment supply chains by inviting the garment industry to set up shop.

> Drawn by newly built industrial parks and a range of financial incentives, manufacturers for some of the world's best-known brands – among them, H&M, Gap, and PVH (Calvin Klein, Izod, Tommy Hilfiger) – employ tens of thousands of Ethiopian workers in a nascent sector the government predicts will one day have billions of dollars in sales.[16]

The government's eagerness to attract foreign investment led it to promote the lowest base wage in any garment-producing country – now set at the equivalent of US$26 per month. On that amount, the mostly female workers cannot afford decent housing, food and transport. Minimum prices for a commodity or the provision of a living wage, whether for cobalt from the Democratic Republic of Congo, for hazelnuts from Turkey or for garments from Ethiopia, provides a safety net for workers. It means that the market-driven race to the bottom in terms of cost is not inextricably linked to a decline in labour standards.

Promoting alternative business models such as cooperatives and worker-owned enterprises is also a public policy option. This would increase the likelihood that created value is shared equitably, while workers gain more control over the production process and over their pay and conditions. Cooperatives and worker-owned enterprises are not new. Farmers have long recognised there is strength in numbers. Cooperatives provide local farmers with economies of scale and enable them to do business on their own terms when dealing with large companies. This can help them to resist unsustainable cost pressures that lead to exploitation, as is evident in supermarket supply chains.[17] Employee ownership also has advantages because modern slavery is far less likely to occur at worker-owned enterprises. Governments can support such alternative business models in various ways; for example, by providing loans with favourable rates, by granting tax advantages or by favouring cooperatives and worker-owned enterprises in public procurement decisions.

Governments should generally ensure that the goods and services they procure are free of modern slavery. Target 12.7 of the United Nations' 2030 Sustainable Development Goals is to 'promote public procurement practices that are sustainable, in accordance with national policies and priorities'. Because of the size of public spending, governments have unmatched leverage to change business practices for the better through their purchasing decisions. Annually, governments across the European Union (EU) spend 14 per cent of national income, or €1.9 trillion, on public procurement.[18] The EU issued three directives in 2014 that encourage the use of social and human rights–related criteria within procurement processes.[19] EU directives are addressed to EU member states, who must give them effect in their domestic law.

> Sweden's county councils spend €13 billion per year via collective procurement. Since 2010, they have used a common code of conduct for suppliers, followed up on by supplier questionnaires and targeted factory audits. A 2015 study found these measures significantly reduced serious labour rights abuses in workshops in Pakistan supplying the councils with surgical instruments, while workers in neighbouring facilities did not experience similar improvements.[20]

Unlike well-known brands, many companies that supply to government are relatively unknown and do not face the same pressure to address the threat of modern slavery. This lack of public pressure on companies can be substituted by demands made by government. Local authorities in Greece are a case in point. Greece has an estimated 89 000 modern-day slaves – or about one in 125 people.[21] Thousands of refugees fleeing war and poverty have arrived in the country since 2015, many of whom are at risk of exploitation. The Athenian municipality has expressed its intention to work solely with suppliers that monitor their supply chains and address modern slavery.[22]

State intervention does not always result in progress, however, and governments also hinder the fight against modern slavery. NGOs are increasingly faced with non-cooperative or even hostile governments. In 2018, Italy turned away ships operated by aid groups that carried migrants from Libya who were rescued at sea. The Italian government argued its actions were intended as an 'anti-trafficking measure'.[23] Human rights campaigners and migrant workers in Thailand were hit with defamation cases after they accused a chicken farm of forced labour. While the Thai court acquitted the campaigners and workers, in another case in 2019, a Thai court upheld a defamation judgment against British human rights activist Andy Hall, ordering him to pay 10 million baht (AU$453 000) in damages to Natural Fruit Co. Ltd, a Thai pineapple company.[24] Hall was sued by Natural Fruit following his research for a 2013 report by Finnish consumer organisation Finnwatch. In it, migrant workers from Myanmar alleged that

Natural Fruit abused them and broke labour laws. It is shocking that criminal defamation laws can be used to threaten human rights defenders and victims of modern slavery for the purpose of protecting corporate reputation.[25] Although modern slavery is rife in Thailand, state intervention has been poor. The labour inspection regime introduced by Thai authorities following modern slavery revelations did not find not a single case of forced labour in 2015.[26]

The state can evidently pull many levers to combat modern slavery. While the government is a powerful actor, its actions to stop forced labour can only come to full fruition if companies and civil society are committed and active participants. Collaboration with companies is vital, as they can act as influential change agents. Business leaders and large companies can use their influence to uphold and diffuse ethical norms. If there is resistance among the business community, even a powerful actor like the government will likely fail to achieve its objectives. Participation of civil society organisations such as trade unions, NGOs and charities is also crucial, because they often provide a voice to marginalised and exploited workers who would otherwise not be heard. More broadly, a healthy civil society consists of conscious consumers and critical citizens who hold companies and government accountable.

Leveraging corporate power

Since many states are hesitant to play an active role, the fight against modern slavery relies heavily on the voluntary efforts of companies. A select few companies have made modern slavery – or rather, the lack thereof – an explicit part of their brand. Two examples are Tony Chocolonely, a Dutch chocolate maker, and Outland Denim, a jeans company from Australia who markets their products as slave-free.[27] Sadly, the majority of companies show wilful ignorance regarding modern slavery in their supply chains. According to Shraysi Tandon, director of an award-winning documentary about forced labour in supply chains[28], modern slavery is seen as a problem that is too difficult and expensive to address. She adds that companies will resort to action 'when their brand or reputation is being threatened'.[29]

Identifying corporate motivations goes a long way towards predicting the failure or success of their approach to modern slavery. Companies that do nothing more than simply following the letter of the law are likely to fall short. In the UK, among companies that report under the *Modern Slavery Act*, disclosures are often inadequate. The scope and quality of disclosures do not reflect effective due diligence processes, and information is not detailed enough to allow monitoring by the state and civil society.[30] In 2017, 43 per cent of companies on the London Stock Exchange did not even bother to report at all, nor did 42 per cent of the top

100 companies that were awarded government contracts.[31] Evidently, the lack of sanctions when failing to report has resulted in many businesses considering compliance with this legislation as something that is discretionary rather than obligatory. This indicates a lack of corporate motivation to deal seriously with the issue.

Apart from complying with the law (or not), companies can have other motivations to address modern slavery. For some companies, such as Tony Chocolonely and Outland Denim, it is because fighting modern slavery is an explicit part of their business model. For many others, motivation comes from the need to manage brand value and company reputation. Arguably, some companies may simply want to 'do the right thing'. Yet, if companies were truly driven by moral incentives, this would have resulted in substantive action. Corporate voluntarism and self-regulation would have resulted in significant progress by now – and this has not been the case. The emphasis on brand value and company reputation can help to explain this. Addressing modern slavery often becomes a means to an end – safeguarding reputation – rather than an end in itself. Consequently, any action that achieves this goal suffices, resulting in the possibility of a symbolic rather than a substantive approach to modern slavery.

The response by companies and industry bodies to modern slavery in the Thai seafood industry is a good example of this. Following global outrage about large seafood companies being implicated in modern slavery, and supermarkets stocking shelves with items produced by means of forced labour, the 'Seafood Taskforce' was created by supermarkets, buyers, retailers and civil society groups to bring transparency and accountability to seafood supply chains. This industry-led multi-stakeholder initiative, consisting of retailers such as Walmart and Costco, large seafood producers including Thai Union Group, and charities such as the World Wildlife Fund, aims to safeguard conditions and wages for fishermen. Yet, this group has failed to make substantial progress and has attracted criticism from other civil society groups. 'Never in my career have I seen a process more focused on talking in hotel rooms in Bangkok rather than actually committing to using their influence to create real change.'[32] The creation of the Seafood Taskforce has been successful in managing public perception, yet Thailand's seafood industry remains infested with modern slavery.[33]

So, what is needed to make companies do better? Modern slavery laws like those introduced in the UK and Australia may generate corporate awareness, but this alone is not enough to change corporate culture. All the modern slavery disclosures in the world will not alone abolish the practice. Is it even realistic to assume that companies will cease unethical but profitable business practices, without being forced to do so through state interference and scrutiny from civil society? There are various ways for companies to be more effective in addressing modern slavery, yet none of these strategies are likely to work unless there is a major change in corporate culture. The dominant view of the primary purpose of companies is that they have a fiduciary obligation to make profits. In other words, it is their main duty to create as much value as possible for their shareholders. This fixation on shareholder value is mirrored in corporate decision-making processes.

For example, the quest to maximise shareholder returns justifies driving down costs through outsourcing and legitimises cutthroat competition among suppliers. As we have seen, such scenarios create ideal conditions for modern slavery to thrive. On Paul Polman's first day as CEO of Unilever in 2009, he did what few companies had or have since done: he eliminated the company's quarterly earnings reports. His argument was that his role was to create long-term value and sustainability for his investors, and this would be hampered rather than enhanced by being too focused on short-term returns.

In considering long-term value and sustainability, it is important for companies to examine whether their own business model and practices may facilitate modern slavery. While doing so, companies must recognise that modern slavery occurs on a continuum that can begin with labour abuses and workers' right violations, such as wage theft and excessive recruitment fees paid to labour hire companies. Regrettably, companies and employer associations tend to downplay these issues; for example, they euphemistically refer to wage theft as 'wage non-compliance' or by lobbying against calls to license labour hire companies. This culture of resistance and the failure to recognise the slippery slope towards modern slavery means that companies will have difficulties in understanding where the risk of modern slavery lies within their own practices. Changes in corporate culture often originate at the top. The Chairman and Managing Director of Konica Minolta Australia, David Cooke, noted, once he became aware of the more than 40 million people enslaved and that some of those are in corporate supply chains, 'I couldn't un-know it'.[34] In his 2019 annual letter to chief executives, Larry Fink, head of BlackRock, the richest investment firm in the world, called for companies to find their social purpose, saying that profits are not inconsistent with purpose.[35] There are costs to continuing to perpetuate a corporate culture that prizes ill-gained, short-term returns over the creation of long-term value: regulatory penalties, exposure for executives – both reputational and legal – risk of shareholder and consumer activism, and risk to the chances of attracting and retaining top talent. However, it is also true that, for some companies, the benefit of employing cheaper suppliers who may use forced labour still outweighs the potential cost of exposure.

While the public-facing aspect of corporate culture may be determined by the CEO, the board of directors and glossy sustainability reports, its everyday manifestation is the cumulative result of countless interactions in the organisational pyramid. In other words, while the company executives may explicitly define and dictate a social purpose, this still needs to be operationalised by people on the ground. The problem with executives saying that 'profits are not inconsistent with social purpose' is that this is not the same as saying that 'profits need to be consistent with social purpose'. Only the latter statement expresses a commitment to doing things differently. The bonus culture in the financial services sector is a good example. This incentivised unethical behaviour, for example, through predatory mortgage lending by American banks in the lead up to the Global Financial Crisis and recently through charging fees to dead people by Australian banks. After several scandals, the industry has vowed to change. Yet if people face the same performance measures as before, then they are likely to replicate their decisions and repeat mistakes.[36] The same is true for procurement managers: if a reduction in cost is their main aim, then their sourcing decisions will remain unchanged.

In such instances, companies will continue to take a reactive approach to modern slavery. They will reap the benefits of cheap (or unpaid) labour and exploitative conditions until abuses are revealed. They will cut and run when modern slavery is exposed, which means that ties with suppliers are severed rather than abuses being remediated. Whether or not a region or industry is prone to modern slavery will not be a relevant consideration up until that point. Conversely, to genuinely do things differently, companies would take a proactive approach; for example, by buyers making long-term commitments to exclusive suppliers or relational sourcing.[37] They would locate operations or source goods from areas with a strong human and labour rights record, including operating or sourcing from a region that supports a living wage, or where organised labour is prevalent. Companies would invest in the training and welfare of workers, including housing. Companies that provide transport, meals and bonuses that incentivise attendance and productivity can reduce turnover rates. Companies would not hinder efforts of their workers or their suppliers' workers to join or establish a union, nor would they lobby against increased human and labour rights protections in export-oriented countries. They would engage regularly with organised labour and community groups to determine a living wage and fair working conditions, and they would improve supply chain transparency by publicly disclosing names and locations of suppliers, something H&M committed to do in 2019. If modern slavery occurs despite all these efforts, companies should provide victims with avenues for redress. Collaboration is key in all this. Working within a multi-stakeholder framework will be more helpful than companies going it alone.

For example, the Bangladesh Accord on Fire and Building Safety was established after the Rana Plaza disaster in Bangladesh in 2013. It brought together international brands and trade unions to work towards a safer garment and textile industry. The Accord is a legally binding agreement that provides for independent factory safety inspections, remediation, an anonymous complaints procedure and health and safety training for workers. The Accord is far from perfect. It does not cover all of Bangladesh's garment factories, and its narrow focus on safety issues means that it can't specifically address broader human rights risks – including modern slavery. Yet, the Accord has set an example of stakeholders working collaboratively to address and remediate workplace risks. Ultimately, while companies may theoretically be able to reduce the risks of modern slavery by themselves, the participation of the state, and civil society in particular, can help to avoid corporate window dressing. Unfortunately, the trend among companies to focus on modern slavery so far appears to be more of a public relations exercise in reaction to scandalous revelations. In what seems to be the majority of cases, when due diligence is performed prior to entering a new market or engaging a supplier, the focus of companies lies on uncovering the potential risk to the corporate image rather than the risk to the workers. Companies, therefore, still have a long way to go in understanding and acting upon human and labour rights risks in their operations and supply chains.

A vibrant and active civil society

It is no coincidence that modern slavery has thrived in an era where many governments have pursued an agenda of trade liberalisation and deregulation of labour markets.

The previous chapters have described the marginalised role of nation-states in safeguarding labour and human rights, and the increased reliance on intervention by non-governmental stakeholders. Concerning the last point, the declining role of traditional institutions is offset by 'the development of issue-oriented mobilizations by groups and individuals outside the mainstream political system'.[38] Put differently, civil society has often stepped into the breach. Civil society includes individuals, not-for-profit groups and organisations that are independent of the government and usually have public good as a mission, such as NGOs, trade unions, academics and faith-based organisations. Some might include business in this definition as a non-state actor, but the economic and political influence of large contemporary companies warrants them being excluded from the definition, as they have become a force in and of themselves.

The shortcomings of existing institutions to address modern slavery has prompted social movements to play a growing role in holding companies and governments to account. In the age of globalisation, civil society can serve as an alternative to traditional institutions that have come under pressure (that is, the state), and as a counter-force to newly dominant institutions (multinational companies). Civil society groups such as trade unions and NGOs generally enjoy strong social standing. They are viewed as working with the public interest in mind rather than being driven by self-interest.[39] Because they are regarded positively, civil society organisations can form a powerful tandem with the media, which allows them to inform the public and shape their expectations. Civil society is a powerful actor in ensuring that companies behave responsibly and are publicly held to account, and has long relied on publicly 'naming and shaming' as a key tactic in putting pressure on companies. Such tactics are most effective when focused on public-facing brands whose reputation is critical.

Earlier chapters detailed the use of such tactics against companies such as Nike and Nestlé. Naming and shaming – which involves persuading stakeholders to exert pressure on the relevant target (for example, a company or government) to curb abuses of rights – has long been an essential tool of the broader human rights movement. While its effectiveness may vary, and its utility is sometimes short-lived, it is a tactic with several purposes. First, it is often important to survivors of human rights abuses that their suffering, and the identities of those responsible for their suffering, should be known. Survivors want to tell their story, want it to be recorded and want the information to be disseminated as widely as possible. Second, detailed and reliable information is needed within countries where abuses have taken place if efforts are to be made to achieve change. The information gathered detailing the extent of labour abuses and modern slavery in global supply chains has been a significant factor in pushing for legislative changes. In France, the establishment of the 2017 'duty of vigilance' law was years in the making, but was hastened by the collapse of the Rana Plaza building in Bangladesh and the exposure of poor working conditions in global garment supply chains. Third, public attention that links abusive practices with a specific company, or even a whole sector, will motivate some companies to at least attempt to address such criticisms and some will be motivated to delve more deeply into their supply chains.

Civil society groups may also enter into corporate partnerships, which sometimes happens following a naming and shaming campaign. An example is the Indonesian Protocol on Freedom of Association. The Protocol was the result of public pressure generated by the Play Fair Campaign, especially around the Beijing Olympics in 2008, and 'is an agreement between five Indonesian unions, six global sportswear brands – Nike, Adidas, Pentland, Puma, New Balance and ASICS – and four major Indonesian footwear manufacturers. In December of 2017 three more brands signed onto the Protocol'.[40] The Protocol is focused on ensuring the workers have the ability to form trade unions and access grievance mechanisms. It provides a monitoring committee with access to a list of all the brands' suppliers, although the list is not public. The Play Fair Campaign then reports publicly whether the brands are meeting their commitments under the Protocol.

In these scenarios, civil society is delivering public services such as labour inspections, traditionally a state function based on context-specific standards, which might be a mix of public and private regulations often devised by a multi-stakeholder group. Even places such as the UK and Australia, which have modern slavery laws, are still largely 'outsourcing enforcement' of those laws to civil society. The idea is that mandatory reporting enables civil society to expose poorly performing companies, who will then get named and shamed into doing the right thing. In such an environment, transparency is absolutely vital. The more information available on global business operations, the more feasible it becomes for non-state actors to hold companies to account. However, this reliance on non-state actors is not without issues. While it can work when governments are unable or unwilling to act, civil society organisations lack state-like enforcement capacity and instruments such as fines and forced inspections, which shows that they cannot fully replace the function of the state to protect labour and human rights.

As the discussion in earlier chapters has revealed, there has been no shortage of corporate social responsibility initiatives that claim to ameliorate a corporation's impact on human rights. It is a positive development that (some) companies and states are now more eager to collaborate with civil society than they were 20 years ago, but not all initiatives are created equal. Worker-driven social responsibility is a relatively new approach in this field for enforcing social standards in supply chains; workers themselves are the driving force behind creating, monitoring and enforcing workplace standards. One example of this approach that we discussed earlier in chapter 4 is the Fair Food campaign initiated by the Coalition of Imokalee Workers, which involves a significant number of seasonal migrant workers who head north annually to pick tomatoes in the US.

Another is the Milk with Dignity program that brings together farm workers, farmers, buyers and consumers to promote workers' rights in the dairy industry in Vermont.[41] Migrant Justice, a Vermont non-profit organisation, established the program in 2014, and the farm workers played a key role in developing the program's standards. In 2017, ice-cream maker Ben & Jerry's signed an agreement with Milk with Dignity to only work with farmers who pay at least the minimum wage and ensure that their suppliers provide adequate housing and rest for their workers. None of these demands seem radical, particularly in a prosperous country like the US, and yet initiatives like this and the Fair Food campaign spent years in development and have met major resistance from companies.

It is unlikely that such initiatives can be replicated in countries where there is not a vibrant and active civil society movement. In general, we should be mindful of leaving the regulation of the business sector entirely to civil society given the inherent risks facing the sector, including lack of funding and resources, threats towards human rights defenders and restrictions on advocacy. This is a key point. In general, any type of enforcement that relies on workers or civil society organisations can only work if they are able to perform their work unhindered. This is where a paradoxical development can be seen. Although governments around the world increasingly rely on civil society to perform this function, we have simultaneously witnessed a global crackdown on civil society. In its 2019 report 'Laws designed to silence: The global crackdown on civil society organizations', Amnesty International highlights the global trend to use restrictive legislation to target human rights defenders. The report shows an alarming global trend in the last decade in which states are introducing and using laws to interfere with the right to freedom of association and to hamper the work of civil society groups and individuals who participate in them.

According to the report, the pace at which this happens is accelerating. Since 2017, almost 40 pieces of legislation have been either put in place or are in the pipeline globally. For example, in the same year that Australia introduced its *Modern Slavery Act*, parliament also passed the *National Security Legislation Amendment (Espionage and Foreign Interference) Act*. This law imposes criminal penalties for sharing what is broadly defined as 'sensitive' information. While the legislation contains certain provisions to protect journalists, it does not contain safeguards to protect whistleblowers who divulge information about human rights abuses or other information of public interest. Nor does it protect human rights defenders or organisations who may discuss human rights concerns with representatives of foreign governments or international human rights mechanisms.

In a similar fashion, the state has been hindering the efforts of organised labour. Organisations fighting for vulnerable workers are increasingly silenced as governments around the world crack down on workers' rights. In 2018, 65 per cent of countries around the world barred workers from the right to establish or join a trade union, 81 per cent violated the right to collective bargaining, while 87 per cent violated the right to strike. The number of countries with arbitrary arrests and detention of workers increased from 44 in 2017 to 59 in 2018, and the number of countries where workers were exposed to murder, physical violence, death threats and intimidation rose from 59 in 2017 to 65 in 2018.[42]

The prospect of exploitation and forced labour diminishes in places where strong worker collectives exist, yet a survey conducted by the International Labour Organization among 1454 companies in global supply chains found that less than a third of workers are covered by a collective agreement.[43] Governments must, therefore, focus on ensuring that workers have labour rights as well as the ability to organise and collectively demand better pay and conditions. The director of Global Labour Justice in the US, a global network of worker and migrant groups, has put it eloquently: 'The opposite of trafficking isn't no trafficking – it is the ability of migrants and workers to organise to demand their rights'.[44]

Shareholder activism and ethical consumption

Social activism and campaigns for workers' rights are not only shaped by NGOs and trade unions, but also by investment and individual purchasing decisions. Ethical investment, also referred to as socially responsible investment, is an instrument used to engage companies over issues of societal concern. Historically, it has been used to influence company behaviour on matters such as the Vietnam War, apartheid in South Africa and the civil rights struggle in the US.[45] In 1970, a shareholder resolution was presented at the annual general meeting of General Motors, in which an activist investor group sought action on the needs of minority workers, the inclusion of women and African Americans on the board of directors, and a 'social audit' of the company's performance with respect to pollution and consumer safety.[46] Although the proposals were all defeated, the campaign brought attention to the issues raised and spurred debate within institutions that held shares in General Motors about their duties and powers as shareholders.

The decisions that investors make each day shape the nature of business and the global market. Investors can intersect with modern slavery in a variety of ways, from (perhaps) unwittingly laundering illicit funds generated from slavery, to investment in businesses engaged in this form of exploitation. There are different ways in which investors might choose to employ financial leverage to influence corporate behaviour. An individual may choose to invest their money in specific funds or stocks that align with their values. Some funds specifically brand themselves as ethical investment funds. One of the best-known ethical investment funds is the Government Pension Fund of Norway, a state-owned investment fund that manages money derived from the country's reserves. Another example is CalPERS, the largest pension fund in the US.[47] These 'sovereign wealth' funds are part of a broader group of institutional investors that dominate global financial markets. The Norwegian Fund is the largest sovereign wealth fund in the world,[48] and was the first large institutional investor to apply ethical criteria to its portfolio.[49] It has a high degree of transparency: it makes public its assessments of corporate conduct with respect to human rights, a practice that has been rare among investors.

In order to avoid profiting from modern slavery, individual and institutional investors should proactively assess the measures taken by the companies they invest in to reduce the risk of modern slavery, and ask companies to increase the transparency of their supply chain. Fortunately, investors increasingly recognise that 'the lack of reliable, accessible information about the human rights track records of individual companies hinders their ability to manage medium- to long-term risks and advance social objectives in an investment context'.[50] Where such risks are not addressed, they can result in legal, reputational and financial repercussions.

In 2015, US marine services company Signal International LLC had to pay US$20 million in compensation to former employees who were victims of human trafficking. The company eventually filed for bankruptcy. Two public pension funds, the Teachers' Retirement System of Alabama and the Employees' Retirement System of Alabama, owned more than 47 per cent of Signal and lost approximately US$70 million.[51]

Financial modelling shows that the hypothetical share price of a company that does not address labour and human rights risks in its supply chains would fall from US$100 to US$49 due to downtime, lost contracts, personnel costs and victim compensation.[52] Data that evaluates corporate social performance is, therefore, becoming increasingly 'valuable'. The NGO Know the Chain has developed a set of indicators, along with investors and the Investor Alliance for Human Rights, to analyse corporate disclosure and performance compared to industry peers and compliance with legislation.[53] Investors should integrate such indicators into investment decision-making. Active ownership should also be encouraged. Investors should ask companies how they create value by reducing business exposure to forced labour, how they are working to ensure (migrant) workers are not exploited, how they engage with workers in their supply chains to empower them to exercise their rights, and whether they have an early warning system and grievance mechanisms in place for when abuses do occur.

At the same time as addressing modern slavery is a matter of making ethical investment decisions, it is also a matter of individuals making sound purchasing decisions. The preceding chapters have shown that modern slavery is an integral part of the economy, and that it is associated with many products and services that we use on a daily basis. It is not uncommon for surveys to be released professing the rise of the ethical consumer.

> A new [2018] report by communications agency Fleishman Hillard Fishburn (FHF) revealed that 93% of the millennial generation want to buy from companies that have purpose, sustainability and environmental stewardship built into their ethos. FHF surveyed 30 sustainability and CSR professionals to gauge public attitudes. The findings echo those of Deloitte, which claimed in 2016 that 56% of millennials will exclude companies that are not operating sustainably from their shopping lists, while 49% will refuse to work for companies that go against their personal ethics.[54]

However, Apple's sales and profits skyrocketed in the years that coincided with an epidemic of worker suicides and other forms of exploitation in its supply chain. This begs the question whether there is a critical mass of ethical consumers that can support the work of civil society and use their own leverage to make companies change.

Indeed, a series of studies on 'The myth of the ethical consumer' provides evidence that while consumers profess a social consciousness in surveys (where there is no cost), they fail to live up to this when their behaviour is examined directly or via structured experimentation.[55] Meaning that other than for a relatively small group of 'activist consumers' or for purchase of niche products, consumers are not necessarily 'walking the talk'.

Thus, it is not clear that consumers are willing to pay higher prices for products made in workplaces where human rights are respected. In part, this reluctance may stem from two things. One is the lack of credible social labelling systems that could provide the consumer with veracity about the specific source of a product and the conditions in which it was made; two, the lack of access to broader consumer-friendly information that provides them with information about the company more generally. There have been significant efforts in recent years to enable consumers to make better purchasing decisions. Following exploitation in the garment industry, the NGO Baptist World Aid has annually published its ethical fashion guide, as part of its 'behind the barcode' project. Companies are awarded grades on the basis of efforts they have undertaken to mitigate the risks of forced labour, child labour and worker exploitation in their supply chains.[56] Similarly, the Corporate Human Rights Benchmark and Oxfam's Behind the Brands offer consumers an insight into the way their favourite brands do business.

Another example is Good on You, an online platform and mobile app that ranks fashion brands. Established by Ethical Consumers Australia, Good on You is a commercial business that is driven by a social mission. It aggregates all the relevant public information available from certification schemes (FairTrade, Global Organic Textile Standard, Cradle to Cradle and many more), from civil society investigations and from brands' own statements. It has plans to include other consumer product categories such as cosmetics and personal care items, homewares and electronics, based on requests from users.

As consumers, we should be more vigilant and learn to ask the right questions to bring modern slavery to light. If you see four people cleaning your vehicle for half an hour at the car wash, for which you have paid the equivalent of the hourly minimum wage, then it is likely that these workers are being exploited. Ask yourself who is benefiting from this arrangement. If they are migrant workers, ask yourself if they can move freely. If they have poor English-language skills, ask yourself if they are aware of their rights. Similarly, if you buy a T-shirt for the price of a cup of coffee, then someone in a garment factory or cotton field has paid the real price for that piece of clothing. If something is too cheap to be true, it usually is. For Karla Jacinto, a Mexican trafficking survivor and activist, changing public perceptions around modern slavery is vital. 'It's not the acts of bad people that hurt me the most', she told the conference. 'It's the indifference of the public.'[57]

Technology to the rescue?

Apps, big data, artificial intelligence and blockchain are examples of technologies that promise to solve the world's problems. For that reason, many organisations have turned to these technologies to address modern slavery. Since it is the UN's goal to end human trafficking and modern slavery by 2030, a comprehensive rather than a piecemeal approach is required. The use of big data can facilitate such an approach. For example, calls to the anti-slavery helpline in the UK are geographically plotted to reveal modern slavery hotspots. An online map allows the public and government to see the percentage of calls from their region.[58] This strategy is also applied globally, with 147 nations having agreed to map practices and count the victims of modern slavery. The gathering of global data using standardised measures creates a more comprehensive and comparable overview of modern slavery. It allows authorities to join the dots and identify causes and patterns.[59] The benefits of such methods are undeniable and there are many possible uses for such large data sets.

Even satellite images can be used to identify modern slavery hotspots. Certain industries associated with forced labour show features that can be spotted from space and can be subjected to automated image analysis. Brick kilns, for example, have a typical oval or circular shape and a central chimney. Smoke shows a kiln is operational. Humans were first used to identify kilns

DATA SHARING

In 2018, information technology company IBM, financial services company Western Union and Europol initiated a data-sharing project. They will use financial information to try and predict human trafficking before it even occurs.[60] The idea is that large amounts of aggregated financial data can be used to identify trends in moving illicit profits from human trafficking and modern slavery. Such patterns of suspicious activity can be identified through artificial intelligence and machine learning, which can then be used in real time to raise red flags and trigger further investigations by law enforcement. Social media has also been used to take on modern slavery. Geo-targeted Facebook ads have engaged communities that are vulnerable to labour exploitation. Advertisements in the UK were aimed at Romanian and Polish communities. Messages were sent in the native language of recipients, advising them of their rights and avenues for recourse.[61]

in satellite images and used for machine learning.[62] Other oppressive industries vulnerable to discovery from space include illegal mining and fish processing. Infra-red images can capture the reflections of newly exposed minerals from freshly dug mines. Camps that process the spoils of illegal fishing sometimes require the clearing of mangrove swamps, a characteristic that can be discerned in satellite images.[63] By trawling through satellite images with visual-processing algorithms, researchers at Nottingham university were able to locate 169 out of the 178 brick kilns across Rajasthan in India. A pilot study concluded that 'contemporary earth observation resources and machine learning methods may be successfully applied to help address slavery from space'.[64]

Big data can also be used to identify exploitative business models. In Australia in 2017, the convenience-store chain 7-Eleven was implicated in a massive wage theft scandal, or what the employers and industry associations have euphemistically rebranded as 'wage non-compliance'. Several 7-Eleven franchisees were found to be underpaying their workers, often paying them correctly for payroll purposes but forcing them to pay back cash. The majority of victims were temporary migrants, many international students, who were in breach of their visa conditions. This made them easy targets for exploitative franchisees. Following the scandal, questions were raised about the influence of the 7-Eleven business model. The payments required from franchisees by the 7-Eleven head office created huge downward cost pressures that ultimately resulted in exploitation. Although having to cope with razor-thin margins does not absolve exploitative employers, it does reveal the structural burdens and the cost pressures generated by the 7-Eleven business model. The use of big data can identify unsustainable business models relatively easily.

This approach is already applied in the Australian cleaning sector. The Cleaning Accountability Framework, a multi-stakeholder initiative aimed at safeguarding social standards in the cleaning sector, uses big data to identify exploitation. As the barrier of entry into this industry is low, many workers come from vulnerable communities and are at risk of falling victim to abusive employers. Years of competitive tendering has resulted in cleaning companies offering unrealistically low rates in an attempt to win contracts to clean office buildings. Rates were then often cut further by subcontracting work to even cheaper service providers. This cutthroat competition intensified workloads and resulted in cleaners being systematically denied entitlements. Based on aggregated data from office buildings across Australia, an acceptable 'productivity rate' was established using statistical methods. The methodology considers factors such as the amount of floor space and the type and number of facilities such as bathrooms and kitchens. In doing so, it can identify when a cleaning contract for a building results in extreme workloads, or when tendering rates are so low that wage payments below the legal minimum are likely.

In the cases of 7-Eleven and the Australian cleaning industry, it is evident that the business models were important factors in enabling labour abuses. The unrealistically thin margins on which 7-Eleven franchisees were expected to operate and the cutthroat competition for cleaning contracts were structural factors that contributed to exploitation.

The use of big data can take such factors into account and help to raise a red flag. It can determine at what point margins become so thin that labour exploitation is highly likely. This method can be used strategically to combat modern slavery: where there is smoke, there is fire. Specifically, a big-data approach can be applied to low-wage industries that have a low barrier of entry and contain groups that are vulnerable to modern slavery. By recognising the broad patterns of modern slavery, big data can help authorities to strategically enforce labour and criminal laws, it allows trade unions to focus their organising efforts, and it aids companies in their risk management process.

Technology may also be used to better engage workers in supply chains. There are a range of digital tools, including SMS, social media, custom apps and message apps, that are being used to enable workers to provide input (often anonymous) on their working conditions. Many of these tools are focused on gathering worker data so that companies might better understand specific issues or complaints. Examples include Worker Connect, Ulula, Laborlink, IM@Sea and GeoPoll.[65] Releasing the potential of such tools to ensure the safety and security of those who use it depends on accessibility of the tool, while the value of information depends on the veracity and trustworthiness of the data that is provided.

Other technological advances focus on enhancing the transparency and traceability of goods sourced through supply chains. Many of the products that we use every day connect us to a range of labour and human rights abuses. Organisations now increasingly look at blockchain technology to make ethical sourcing decisions. Heralded as the new operating system for society, blockchain technology – or simply, blockchain – can record transactions of anything of value. A blockchain is best envisaged as an online and public ledger. Once a transaction occurs, a permanent and immutable record detailing that transaction is created after being validated by participants in the network. These records are called blocks and are chained together chronologically. Although designed to record Bitcoin transactions, blockchain is increasingly used to prove the integrity of commodities. Simply put, in supply chains, blockchain creates a record from production to consumption, which verifies the source and traces the journey of a product.

For example, together with technology partners and a tuna fishing company, the World Wildlife Fund is piloting blockchain technology to track tuna from 'bait to plate'. Scanning tuna packaging tells consumers when and where it was caught. The idea is that you can be sure you are buying fish that is sustainably caught and free of slave labour. Blockchain is also being used to track a range of other goods, including cotton, fashion, coffee and organically farmed products. Companies such as Ford and IBM are experimenting with blockchain to track cobalt. This mineral is used to create batteries and is in high demand now that the market for electric vehicles is growing. As discussed in chapter 2, around two-thirds of the world's cobalt is sourced from the Democratic Republic of Congo, infamous for its conflict minerals. About one-fifth of cobalt is mined informally by thousands of impoverished people. Blockchain could be used to track cobalt from mine to battery. As the cobalt moves through the supply chain, it would be tracked in the blockchain. Ethically sourced cobalt is recorded and would not be mixed with cobalt from slave labour. This way, companies and customers would know if their phone or car battery is tainted.

While the use of blockchain in supply chains has great potential, implementation is at an early stage. As such, the anticipated transformative effects to ensure ethical sourcing and production are still to be realised, and little is known about potential unintended effects. Such challenges must be anticipated if society is to truly benefit from blockchain technology. For example, a key element of blockchain is the 'consensus protocol'. This dictates who gets to validate a transaction, including information about the conditions in which goods were produced. This protocol can take various forms. It can include all, a majority, a select few or a random selection of supply chain participants. Worryingly, there is no guarantee that workers get a voice in the validation process, which seems especially unlikely if they are marginalised or oppressed. Another issue is the social standard that a blockchain upholds. As there are several blockchain platforms, the social standards that underpin them may differ. As with existing sustainability certification for goods such as coffee, a range of competing sustainability standards may emerge, some of which may be less robust.

Furthermore, it is questionable whether we can truly trust the link between a 'block' and its material reality. Given the size and worth of the dark economy, finding a way to insert goods emanating from modern slavery into the blockchain is lucrative. Although immutable once recorded, the integrity of blockchain data is dependent on human factors and so is vulnerable to inaccuracies or fraud. Blockchain could therefore potentially be used to sanitise goods. Finally, blockchain may create a digital divide. Given the novelty and complexity of this technology, smaller suppliers – especially those in the developing world – may be left out. Its use may further marginalise communities by creating a barrier to enter the market. It is not a given that people who slave away to source the minerals used in mobile phones and electric cars will benefit from blockchain.

Finally, technology that enables the collection and

storage of data on a worker's hours and location creates potential privacy and security risks. This raises questions 'about how to protect worker data from interception or surveillance, and ensure the data collected does not trigger employer/recruiter retaliation or discrimination, coercion, or state immigration enforcement in the case of unauthorised work'.[66]

Despite these challenges, the potential for blockchain technology in supply chains is clear. As a transparency tool it can – at least in theory – record every transaction of value and allow for insights into the provenance of goods. It would be a mistake to hype up blockchain as something much more than that. While its application enables traceability, we cannot address the myriad factors underlying modern slavery by recording transactions in a blockchain. Modern slavery is an issue that requires intervention from governments, intragovernmental organisations, civil society, businesses and consumers. Big data, artificial intelligence and blockchain can only facilitate this intervention. There is no quick technological fix for a complex social problem.

In summary

The challenges to prevent, reduce and redress modern slavery are many. It is a problem on a massive scale, but it is local at the same time. The only way to strategically address it is by breaking it down into manageable pieces. What are the key steps that we should be taking and who is in the best position to take them? Put differently, what can be done, or be done better, by governments, international organisations, brands, suppliers, investors, consumers, civil society and workers to tackle the problem and how can we work together?

One of the first challenges is to accurately define the problem, as this will affect the actions taken to address it. The lack of harmonisation around the definition of modern slavery means that there will inevitably be questions as to the scale and scope of the data. This makes it difficult to assess the (potential) effectiveness of different measures taken to address the problem.

Modern slavery sits on a continuum of exploitation, it should not and cannot be addressed in isolation. In our bid to manage, reduce and eliminate modern slavery, we need to first acknowledge the larger contextual problems from which it emerges. We should treat the symptoms and the causes. In our earlier discussion, we made apparent that there are several key factors that contribute to an increasing number of workers trapped in modern slavery. We have talked about the extreme cost pressures in certain business models, the international fragmentation of production, the changing nature of employment relations, the unprecedented power of large corporations, and the lack of effective regulation to address labour exploitation around the world. Failure to conceptualise and address modern slavery holistically will not result in the systemic change that is needed.

Another problem is the lack of transparency and visibility. The new modern slavery laws mandate disclosure on corporate efforts to address modern slavery and this is an important first step in addressing modern slavery. But there is a significant data gap because most of the world's corporate supply chains are not transparent. Companies have long been reluctant to disclose what they consider commercially sensitive information about their supply chains. It was only in 2019 that companies such as H&M and Nestlé have agreed to provide more precise location data on the fields and factories from which they source their goods. The modern slavery laws in places such as the UK and Australia are a useful first step in uncovering opaque supply chains, and while transparency is key, it cannot be the end game. Modern slavery laws must continue to evolve to include both preventative and remedial measures, they require the provision of more specific data around the sourcing of goods and services, and the laws we have must be adequately enforced.

What is evident is that addressing modern slavery requires a focus on two things: collaboration and connectivity. Collaboration means there will be multiple players using multiple mechanisms to take both individual and collaborative actions. Governments must accept their regulatory role, and craft and enforce new laws that address modern slavery. It is not acceptable for governments to simply 'let business be business'. Similarly, it is no longer enough for companies to deny that there is a problem or think that the production of glossy sustainability reports will provide a solution. Consumers, investors and civil society organisations must continue to demand more information and use what leverage they have to pressure both companies and governments to change course as required. And all of these groups need to collaborate in pursuit of these goals.

Connectivity means that all of us need to truly understand and educate ourselves about the connection between our actions (including our purchases, investments or inaction – our failure to ask questions) and modern slavery. Modern slavery seems like an abstract and distant concept to many, but it is connected to our daily lives. We need to better educate ourselves about what modern slavery is, how it evolves and, importantly, how our often small decisions can affect the lives of many. Modern slavery can affect people of any age, gender or race. It can be a million miles away or in the next suburb. Together, we can each take actions, small and large, to eradicate it.

Notes

Chapter 1—Modern slavery

1 Sustainable Development Solutions Network, 'Indicators and a monitoring framework: Launching a data revolution for the Sustainable Development Goal 8.7', *United Nations*, 2012, <indicators.report/targets/8-7>.

2 International Labour Organization and Walk Free Foundation, *Global Estimates of Modern Slavery: Forced Labour and Forced Marriage* (Report), 19 September 2017, <www.ilo.org/global/publications/books/WCMS_575479/lang--en/index.htm>.

3 A Guterres, 'Message of United Nations Secretary-General on the International Day Against Trafficking in Persons', *United Nations*, 2018, <www.unodc.org/unodc/en/press/releases/2018/July/message-of-united-nations-secretary-general-on-the-international-day-against-trafficking-in-persons.html>.

4 Cardinal V Nichols, 'Slaves on our streets: How the Catholic Church is working with police to bring an end to modern slavery', *The Independent*, 2017, <www.independent.co.uk/voices/slaves-on-our-streets-cardinal-vincent-nichols-catholic-church-pope-francis-modern-slavery-sex-a7945836.html>.

5 P Peachey, 'Human traffickers' victims "branded like cattle"', *The Independent*, 2014, <www.independent.co.uk/news/uk/crime/human-traffickers-victims-branded-like-cattle-9763468.html>.

6 A search was performed in Factiva, a database consisting of more than 32 000 worldwide news sources; Factiva, 'Global news database and licensed content', *Dow Jones*, <www.dowjones.com/products/factiva/>.

7 P Manning, 'The slave trade: The formal demographics of a global system', *Social Science History*, vol. 14, no. 2, 1990, pp. 255–79, cited in JE Inikori & SL Engerman (eds), *The Atlantic Slave Trade: Effects on Economies, Societies and Peoples in Africa, the Americas, and Europe*, Duke University Press, Durham, 1992, 117–44.
8 M Tutton, '40 million slaves in the world, finds new report', *CNN*, 2017, <edition.cnn.com/2017/09/19/world/global-slavery-estimates-ilo/index.html>.
9 Global Slavery Index, 'Country studies: United Kingdom', *The Global Slavery Index*, 2018, <www.globalslaveryindex.org/2018/findings/country-studies/united-kingdom/>, Global Slavery Index, 'Country studies: Australia', *The Global Slavery Index*, 2018, <www.globalslaveryindex.org/2018/findings/country-studies/australia/>.
10 U. Gronniosaw, *A Narrative of the Most Remarkable Particulars in the Life of James Albert Ukawsaw Gronniosaw, an African Prince, as Related by Himself*, 1772.
11 A Kelly & K Hodal, '"I slept on the floor in a flat near Harrods": Stories of modern slavery', *The Guardian*, 2017, <www.theguardian.com/global-development/2017/jul/29/slept-floor-flat-near-harrods-stories-modern-slavery>.
12 Joint Standing Committee on Foreign Affairs, Defence and Trade, Parliament of Australia, *Hidden in Plain Sight: An Inquiry into Establishing a Modern Slavery Act in Australia*, August 2017.
13 Joint Standing Committee on Foreign Affairs, 2017.
14 A Crane, 'Modern slavery as a management practice: Exploring the conditions and capabilities for human exploitation', *Academy of Management Review*, vol. 38, no. 1, 2013, pp. 49–69.
15 N Elbagir, R Razek, A Platt, & B Jones, 'People for sale: Where lives are auctioned for $400', *CNN*, 2017, <edition.cnn.com/2017/11/14/africa/libya-migrant-auctions/index.html>.
16 H Lewis, P Dwyer, S Hodkinson & L Waite, *Precarious Lives: Forced Labour, Exploitation and Asylum*, The Policy Press, Bristol, 2015, 152–3.
17 L Berg & B Farbenblum, *Wage Theft in Australia: Findings of the National Temporary Migrant Work Survey*, (Report, November 2017), <apo.org.au/system/files/120406/apo-nid120406-483146.pdf>.
18 A Ferguson & S Danckert, 'Revealed: How 7 Eleven is ripping off its workers', *Sydney Morning Herald*, 2015, <www.smh.com.au/interactive/2015/7-eleven-revealed/>.
19 C Meldrum-Hanna, A Russell, & M Christodoulo, 'Labour

exploitation, slave-like conditions found on farms supplying biggest supermarkets', *Australian Broadcasting Corporation*, 2015, <www.abc.net.au/news/2015-05-04/supermarkets-food-outlets-exploit-black-market-migrant-workers/6441496>.

20 United Voice, Submission No 116 to Joint Standing Committee on Foreign Affairs, Defence and Trade, *Parliamentary Inquiry into Establishing a Modern Slavery Act in Australia*, 5 May 2017, <www.aph.gov.au/DocumentStore.ashx?id=3df1ff45-d123-4dd6-a30c-63b86bb93c60&subId=511071>.

21 Fair Work Ombudsman, 'Penalties of $447,300 and $223,000 back-pay ordered after workers treated as "slaves"', *Fair Work Ombudsman*, 2017, <www.fairwork.gov.au/about-us/news-and-media-releases/2017-media-releases/june-2017/20170806-gps-penalty>.

22 *Fair Work Ombudsman v Grouped Property Services Pty Ltd (No 2)* [2017] FCA 557.

23 Fair Work Ombudsman, 'Harvest Trail Inquiry', *Fair Work Ombudsman*, 2018, <www.fairwork.gov.au/how-we-will-help/helping-the-community/campaigns/national-campaigns/harvest-trail-inquiry>.

24 C Knaus, 'ACT massage parlour accused of mistreatment, control of Filipino workers', *Canberra Times*, 2016, <www.canberratimes.com.au/national/act/act-massage-parlour-accused-of-mistreatment-control-of-filipino-workers-20160630-gpvbfk.html>.

25 A Jardine, 'Modern slavery: Migrants forced to work gruelling hours at hand car washes', *The Conversation*, 18 October 2018, <theconversation.com/modern-slavery-migrants-forced-to-work-gruelling-hours-at-hand-car-washes-105165>.

26 A Jardine, A Trautrims, & E Keyway, 'Labour exploitation in hand car washes. Office of the Independent Anti-Slavery Commissioner and the University of Nottingham's Rights Lab', *Anti-Slavery Commissioner*, 2018, <www.antislaverycommissioner.co.uk/media/1238/labour-exploitation-in-hand-car-washes.pdf>.

27 S Elks, 'UK rejects calls to license car washes to prevent worker abuses', *Thomson Reuters Foundation News*, 2019, <news.trust.org/item/20190131235247-gi600/>,

28 F Lawrence & E McSweeney, 'UK police rescue nine suspected victims of slavery from British trawlers', *The Guardian*, 12 December 2017, <www.theguardian.com/world/2017/dec/12/uk-police-rescue-nine-suspected-victims-of-slavery-from-british-trawlers>.

29 Migrant Rights Centre Ireland, 'Migrant Rights Centre Ireland meets with government taskforce on situation of undocumented migrant fishermen', *Migrant Rights Centre Ireland*, 12 November 2014, <www.mrci.ie/press-centre/migrant-rights-centre-ireland-meets-with-government-taskforce-on-situation-of-undocumented-migrant-fishermen/>.

30 F Lawrence & E McSweeney, 'Non-EEA migrants on Irish trawlers gain new immigration rights', *The Guardian*, 2019, <www.theguardian.com/world/2019/apr/22/non-eea-migrants-on-irish-trawlers-gain-new-immigration-rights>

31 S Elks, 'Migrant fishing workers in Ireland to get protections against slavery, *Thomson Reuters Foundation News*, 2019, <www.reuters.com/article/us-ireland-labor-fishing/migrant-fishing-workers-in-ireland-to-get-protections-against-slavery-idUSKCN1RZ1L9>.

32 O. Equiano, *The Interesting Narrative of the Life of Olaudah Equiano, Or Gustavus Vassa, The African, Written by Himself*, 1789.

33 Al Jazeera, 'Food chain slaves. Slavery: A 21st century evil', Al Jazeera, 2016, <www.aljazeera.com/programmes/slaverya21stcenturyevil/2011/10/201110108583163675.html>

34 United States Department of Labor, 'List of goods produced by child labor or forced labor', *United States Department of Labor*, 2018, <www.dol.gov/agencies/ilab/reports/child-labor/list-of-goods>.

35 D Weil, *The Fissured Workplace: Why Work Became so Bad for so Many and What Can Be Done to Improve It*, Harvard University Press, Cambridge, MA, 2017.

36 M Boersma, *Do No Harm? Procurement of Medical Goods by Australian Companies and Government*, March 2017, <www.anmf.org.au/documents/Do_No_Harm_Report.pdf>.

37 International Labour Organization, 'ILO says forced labour generates annual profits of US$150 billion', *International Labour Organization*, 2014, <www.ilo.org/global/about-the-ilo/newsroom/news/WCMS_243201/lang--en/index.htm>.

38 S Kara, *Modern Slavery: A Global Perspective*, Columbia University Press, New York, 2017.

39 World Bank, 'Decline of global extreme poverty continues but has slowed', 2018, <www.worldbank.org/en/news/press-release/2018/09/19/decline-of-global-extreme-poverty-continues-but-has-slowed-world-bank>.

40 International Labour Organization, 'Profits and poverty: The economics of forced labour (Forced labour, modern slavery and

human trafficking)', *International Labour Organization*, 2014, <www.ilo.org/wcmsp5/groups/public/---ed_norm/-declaration/documents/publication/wcms_243391.pdf>.

41 T Piketty, *Capital in the Twenty-First Century*, Harvard University Press, Cambridge, MAs, 2014.

42 International Labour Organization, *Global Wage Report 2016/17: Wage Inequality in the Workplace*, 15 December 2016, <www.ilo.org/global/ www.ilo.org/wcmsp5/groups/public/---dgreports/---dcomm/---publ/documents/publication/wcms_537846.pdf>.

43 J Stanford, 'The declining labour share in Australia: Definition, measurement, and international comparisons', *Journal of Australian Political Economy*, vol. 81, 2018, pp. 11–32.

44 International Labour Organization, International Monetary Fund, Organisation for Economic Co-operation and Development, & World Bank Group, *Inequality and Labour Income Share in G20 Countries: Trends, Impacts and Causes*, 3–4 September 2015, <www.oecd.org/g20/topics/employment-and-social-policy/Income-inequality-labour-income-share.pdf>.

45 D Hardoon, R Fuentes-Nieva, & S Ayele, 'An economy for the 1%: How privilege and power in the economy drive extreme inequality and how this can be stopped', *Oxfam International*, 2016, p. 44 <www.oxfam.org/sites/www.oxfam.org/files/file_attachments/bp210-economy-one-percent-tax-havens-180116-en_0.pdf>.

46 DAV Pimentel, IM Aymar & M Lawson, *Reward Work, not Wealth*, January 2018, <d1tn3vj7xz9fdh.cloudfront.net/s3fs-public/file_attachments/bp-reward-work-not-wealth-220118-en.pdf>.

47 S Sassen, 'The global city: Introducing a concept', *Brown Journal of World Affairs*, vol. 11, no. 2, 2005, pp. 27–43.

48 TL Friedman, 'It's a flat world, after all', *The New York Times*, 2005, <www.nytimes.com/2005/04/03/magazine/its-a-flat-world-after-all.html>.

49 B Keeley, 'International migration: The human face of globalisation', Organisation for Economic Co-operation and Development Publishing, 2009, <www.oecd.org/insights/43568302.pdf>.

50 M Czaika & H Haas, 'The globalization of migration: Has the world become more migratory?', *International Migration Review*, vol. 48, no. 2, 2014, pp. 283–323.

51 B Doherty & N Evershed, 'The changing shape of Australia's immigration policy', *The Guardian*, 2018, <www.theguardian.com/australia-news/2018/mar/24/australias-fierce-immigration-debate-is-about-to-get-louder>.

52 M McCarthy, 'Ripped off, bullied and harassed: Workers "bonded like slaves", investigation finds', *Australian Broadcasting Network*, 2018, <www.abc.net.au/news/rural/2018-06-27/workplace-watchdog-investigation-into-labour-exploitation/9911710>.

53 L Berg & B Farbenblum, 'Wage theft in Australia: Findings of the National Temporary Migrant Work Survey', *Analysis & Policy Observatory*, 2017, <apo.org.au/system/files/120406/apo-nid120406-483146.pdf>.

54 International Organisation for Migration, Submission No 57 to Joint Standing Committee on Foreign Affairs, Defence and Trade, *Parliamentary Inquiry into Establishing a Modern Slavery Act in Australia*, 28 April 2017, <www.aph.gov.au/DocumentStore.ashx?id=a85ca4c3-e280-4ba1-a70d-d6d308d4f896&subId=510671>.

55 A Kelly & K Hodal, 2017.

56 O. Cugoano, *Thoughts and Sentiments on the Evil and Wicked Traffic of the Slavery and Commerce of the Human Species*, 1787.

57 Scottish Government, 'Publication: Factsheet United Nations Treaties Ratified by the UK', 2016, <www.gov.scot/publications/united-nations-treaties-ratified-by-the-uk/>; Australian Attorney General's Department, 'International human rights system', <www.ag.gov.au/RightsAndProtections/HumanRights/Pages/International-Human-Rights-System.aspx>.

58 Organisation for Economic Co-operation and Development, 'Labour Standards and Economic Integration', 1994, pp. 137–66, <www.oecd.org/els/emp/2409984.pdf>.

59 J Harrison, M Barbu, L Campling, B Richardson & A Smith, 'Governing labour standards through free trade agreements: Limits of the European Union's trade and sustainable development chapters', *Journal of Common Market Studies*, vol. 57, no. 2, 2018, pp. 1–18, <onlinelibrary.wiley.com/doi/full/10.1111/jcms.12715>.

60 RB Davies & KC Vadlamannati, 'A race to the bottom in labor standards? An empirical investigation', *Journal of Development Economics*, vol. 103, 2013, pp. 1–14.

61 DJ Doorey, 'The transparent supply chain: From resistance to implementation at Nike and Levi Strauss', *Journal of Business Ethics*, vol. 103, no. 4, 2011, pp. 587–603.

62 RM Locke, *The Promise and Limits of Private Power: Promoting Labor Standards in a Global Economy*, Cambridge University Press, Cambridge, 2013.

63 LE Bernal-Verdugo, D Furceri, & DM Guillaume, 'Labor market flexibility and unemployment: New empirical evidence of static

and dynamic effects', *Comparative Economic Studies*, vol. 54, no. 2, 2012, pp. 251–73; S Leonardi, & R Pedersini (eds), *Multi-employer Bargaining under Pressure: Decentralisation Trends in Five European countries*, European Trade Union Institute, Brussels, 2018.

64 A Kalleberg, *Good Jobs, Bad Jobs, The rise of Polarized and Precarious Employment Systems in the United States, 1970s to 2000s*, Russell Sage Foundation, New York, 2011; K Stone, 'Flexibilization, globalization, and privatization: Three challenges to labour rights in our time', *Osgoode Hall Law Journal*, vol. 44, no. 1, 2006, pp. 77–104.

65 B France, 'Labour compliance to exploitation and the abuses in-between', Focus on Labour Exploitation (FLEX) and the Labour Exploitation Advisory Group (LEAG), August 2016, <www.labourexploitation.org/sites/default/files/publications/LEAG%20position%20paper%2001.pdf>; A Broughton, M Green, C Rickard, S Swift et al, 'Precarious employment in Europe: Patterns, trends and policy strategies (Policy Department A: Economic and Scientific Policy)', European Parliament, 2016, <www.europarl.europa.eu/RegData/etudes/STUD/2016/587285/IPOL_STU(2016)587285_EN.pdf>.

66 P Bourdieu, *Firing Back: Against the Tyranny of the Market*, trans. L Wacquant, The New Press, New York, 2003, p. 23.

67 P Bourdieu, *Acts of Resistance: Against the Tyranny of the Market*, trans. R Nice, The New Press, New York, 1998, p. 85.

68 PG Standing, *The Precariat: The New Dangerous Class*, Bloomsbury Academic, London, 2016.

69 D Brady, AS Fullerton & JM Cross, 'More than just nickels and dimes: A cross-national analysis of working poverty in affluent democracies', *Social Problems*, vol. 57, no. 4, 2010, pp. 559–85.

70 M Castells, *End of Millennium: The Information Age: Economy, Society, and Culture*, John Wiley & Sons, 2nd edn, vol. 3, 2010, p. 164.

71 P Karp & G Hutchens, 'Neoliberalism has caused "misery and division", Bernie Fraser says', *The Guardian*, 2018, <www.theguardian.com/business/2018/oct/17/neoliberalism-has-caused-misery-and-division-bernie-fraser-says>.

72 International Monetary Fund, 2019.

73 P Pattisson, 'Balfour Beatty and Interserve accused of migrant worker labour abuses in Qatar', *The Guardian*, 2016, <www.theguardian.com/global-development/2016/apr/13/balfour-beatty-interserve-accused-migrant-worker-labour-abuses-qatar>.

74 Human Rights Watch, *World Report: Events of 2013*, 2014, <www.hrw.org/world-report/2014>.

75 P Pattisson, 'Migrants claim recruiters lured them into forced labour at top Qatar hotel', *The Guardian*, 2018, <www.theguardian.com/global-development/2018/oct/29/agents-duped-us-into-forced-labour-at-top-qatar-hotel-say-migrant-workers-marsa-malaz-kempinski>.

76 International Trade Union Confederation, *The Case Against Qatar; Host of the FIFA 2022 World Cup*, March 2014, <www.ituccsi.org/IMG/pdf/the_case_against_qatar_en_web170314.pdf>.

77 O Gibson, 'Migrant workers suffer "appalling treatment" in Qatar World Cup stadiums, says Amnesty', *The Guardian*, 2016, <www.theguardian.com/global-development/2016/mar/31/migrant-workers-suffer-appalling-treatment-in-qatar-world-cup-stadiums-says-amnesty>.

78 Amnesty International, 'Qatar World Cup of shame', 2016, <www.amnesty.org/en/latest/campaigns/2016/03/qatar-world-cup-of-shame/>.

79 Human Rights Watch, 'Qatar: End all migrant worker exit visas', 2018, <www.hrw.org/news/2018/09/06/qatar-end-all-migrant-worker-exit-visas>.

80 J Liew, 'World Cup workers are not workers, they are slaves, and they are building mausoleums, not stadiums', *The Independent*, 2017, <www.independent.co.uk/sport/football/international/world-cup-2022-qatars-workers-slaves-building-mausoleums-stadiums-modern-slavery-kafala-a7980816.html>.

81 'Asia's looming labour shortage', *The Economist*, 2017, <www.economist.com/asia/2017/02/11/asias-looming-labour-shortage>.

82 World Bank, 'High growth in Cambodia expected to continue', 2018, <www.worldbank.org/en/news/press-release/2018/05/10/high-growth-in-cambodia-expected-to-continue-world-bank>.

83 J Ferrie, 'Cambodia construction boom built on 'blood bricks' and slavery – report', *Reuters*, 2018, <af.reuters.com/article/commoditiesNews/idAFL8N1WW34K>.

84 K Brickell, L Parsons, N Natarajan & S Chann, 'Blood bricks: Untold stories of modern slavery and climate change from Cambodia', *Project Blood Bricks*, 2018, <www.projectbloodbricks.org/s/Blood-bricks-high-res-v2.pdf>.

85 TM Li, 'To make live or let die? Rural dispossession and the protection of surplus populations', *Antipode*, vol. 41, no. 1, 2010, pp. 66–93.

86 A Roy, *Poverty Capital: Microfinance and the Making of Development*, Routledge, New York, 2010.

87 M. Prince, *The History of Mary Prince, a West Indian Slave. Related by Herself. With a Supplement by the Editor. To Which Is Added, the Narrative of Asa-Asa, a Captured African*, 1831.

88 B Fernando, *In Contempt of Fate*, Bearo Publishing, Merrimac, Massachusetts, 2013.

89 D Boyd, K Brickell, D Brown, C Ives, N Natarajan & L Parsons, 'Modern slavery, environmental destruction and climate change: Fisheries, field, forests and factories', *Project Blood Bricks*, 2018, <www.projectbloodbricks.org/s/28229-Rights_Lab_A4_Report_Sept_V5.pdf>.

90 I Hunter & LD Pietro, 'The terrible truth about your tin of Italian tomatoes', *The Guardian*, 2017, <www.theguardian.com/global-development/2017/oct/24/the-terrible-truth-about-your-tin-of-italian-tomatoes>.

91 F Lawrence, 'Spain's salad growers are modern-day slaves, say charities', *The Guardian*, 2011, <www.theguardian.com/business/2011/feb/07/spain-salad-growers-slaves-charities>.

92 K McVeigh, 'Migrant crisis triggers heightened risk of slavery in EU supply chains, say analysts', *The Guardian*, 2017, <www.theguardian.com/global-development/2017/aug/10/migrant-crisis-triggers-heightened-risk-of-slavery-in-eu-supply-chains-say-analysts>.

93 L Reynolds, 'Modern slavery in Australia is hiding in plain sight', *Huffington Post*, 2017, <www.huffingtonpost.com.au/linda-reynolds/modern-slavery-in-australia-is-hiding-in-plain-sight_a_22114200/>.

94 A Sereni, 'Modern slavery victims drown in increasingly hostile bureaucratic system', *Thomson Reuterns Foundation News*, 2019, <news.trust.org/item/20190118160913-pbo2n/>.

95 Australian Associated Press, 'Illegal Perth workers crammed into houses', *Yahoo News*, 2017, <au.news.yahoo.com/illegal-wa-workers-crammed-into-houses-35465869.html>

96 B Brook, 'Wage theft: Workers in Australia owed at least $1 billion in lost pay', *News*, 2018, <www.news.com.au/finance/work/at-work/new-research-reveals-at-least-1-billion-owed-in-lost-pay-to-workers-in-australia/news-story/9d70c2d61cdab90a7323c11416df51b7>; D Peetz, 'Self-employment and casual work aren't increasing but so many jobs are insecure – what's going on?', *The Conversation*, 2017, <theconversation.com/self-employment-and-casual-work-arent-increasing-but-so-many-jobs-are-insecure-whats-going-on-100668>; J Eyers, 'ASIC warns banks on credit card debt', *Australian Financial Review*, 2018, <www.afr.com/

business/banking-and-finance/asic-warns-banks-on-credit-card-debt-20180703-h126vr>; P Davidson, P Saunders, B Bradbury & M Wong, 'Poverty in Australia 2018', *Australian Council of Social Service*, 2018, <www.acoss.org.au/wp-content/uploads/2018/10/ACOSS_Poverty-in-Australia-Report_Web-Final.pdf>.

97 Made in a Free World's online tool: <slaveryfootprint.org/>.

Chapter 2—Global supply chains

1 J Dowling, 'The death of the Australian built car', *The Sydney Morning Herald*, 2015, <www.smh.com.au/business/the-economy/who-killed-the-car-industry-20151112-gkx1c8.html>.

2 A ten Kate, I Schipper, V Kiezebrink & M Remmers, 'Beauty and a beast: Child labour in India for sparkling cars and cosmetics', Centre for Research on Multinational Corporations and SOMO, 2016, <www.somo.nl/wp-content/uploads/2016/05/Beauty-and-a-Beast.pdf>.

3 A Banerji, 'Firms urged to follow Mercedes-Benz in Indian mica supply transparency', *Reuters*, 2018, <uk.reuters.com/article/india-auto-mica-idUKL8N1U124K>.

4 'Slave labor persists in Amazon charcoal works: ICC', *Reuters*, 2007, <www.reuters.com/article/us-brazil-slaves-idUSN2743662520070827>.

5 E Hale, 'Ford, GM and BMW linked to illegal logging and slave labour in Brazil' *The Guardian*, 2012 <www.theguardian.com/environment/2012/may/17/ford-gm-bmw-logging-brazil>.

6 S Boseley, 'App sounds alarm for slavery at UK hand carwash sites', *The Guardian*, 2019 <www.theguardian.com/world/2019/apr/07/app-sounds-alarm-for-slavery-at-uk-hand-carwash-sites>.

7 T Wright & N Toscano, 'Armed police remove ship's Australian crew, escort replacements aboard', *The Sydney Morning Herald*, 2016, <www.smh.com.au/national/armed-police-remove-ships-australian-crew-escort-replacements-aboard-20160205-gmml2y.html>.

8 Nautilus International, 'Modern slavery 'alive and kicking' in the maritime industry', *Nautilus*, 2018, <www.nautilusint.org/en/news-insight/press_centre/modern-slavery-alive-and-kicking-in-the-maritime-industry/>.

9 International Transport Federation, 'Modern slavery in UK waters "cannot be tolerated"', *International Transport Federation*, 2017, <www.itfglobal.org/fr/news-events/press-releases/2017/july/modern-slavery-in-uk-waters-cannot-be-tolerated/>.

10 K De Backer & S Miroudot, 'Mapping global value chains', OECD, Paris, 2012, <www.oecd.org/dac/aft/mappingglobalvaluechains_web_usb.pdf>.
11 United Nations Conference on Trade and Development (ed.), *Global Value Chains: Investment and Trade for Development*, United Nations, New York, 2013.
12 International Labour Organization, 'World Employment and Social Outlook 2015: The Changing Nature of Jobs (Report)', 2015, <www.ilo.org/global/research/global-reports/weso/2015-changing-nature-of-jobs/WCMS_368626/lang--en/index.htm>.
13 International Trade Union Confederation, 'Scandal: Inside the Global Supply Chains of 50 Top Companies', 2016, <www.ituc-csi.org/frontlines-report-2016-scandal>.
14 Friends of the Earth Europe, Heinrich Boll Foundation & Rosa Luxemburg Foundation, 'Agrifood atlas: Facts and figures about the corporations that control what we eat', *Heinrich Böll Foundation*, 2017, <www.boell.de/en/2017/10/26/agrifood-atlas-facts-and-figures-about-corporations-control-what-we-eat>.
15 D Vaughan-Whitehead & LP Caro, 'Purchasing practices and working conditions in global supply chains: Global survey results (fact sheet)', *International Labour Organization*, 2017, <www.ilo.org/travail/info/fs/WCMS_556336/lang--en/index.htm>.
16 R Willoughby & T Gore, 'Ripe for change: Ending human suffering in supermarket supply chains', *Oxfam*, 2018, <oxfamilibrary.openrepository.com/bitstream/10546/620418/4/cr-ripe-for-change-supermarket-supply-chains-210618-en.pdf>.
17 T Clarke & M Boersma, 'Global corporations and global value chains: The disaggregation of corporations?' in T Clarke, J O'Brien & C RT O'Kelley (eds), *The Oxford Handbook of the Corporation*, Oxford University Press, Oxford, 2019, pp. 318–65.
18 International Labour Organization, *Non-standard Employment Around the World: Understanding Challenges, Shaping Prospects*, International Labour Office, Geneva, 2016.
19 S Barrientos, 'Corporate purchasing practices in global production networks: A socially contested terrain', *Geoforum*, vol. 44, 2013, pp. 44–51.
20 N Bhalla, R Chandran & A Nagaraj, 'Blood mica: Deaths of child workers in India's mica "ghost" mines covered up to keep industry alive', *Thomson Reuters Foundation*, 2016, <news.trust.org/shorthand/mica/>.
21 A Crane, G LeBaron, K Phung, L Behbahani & J Allain,

'Innovations in the business models of modern slavery: The dark side of business model innovation', *Academy of Management Proceeding*, vol. 1, pp. 13 381–7.

22 A Crane, G LeBaron, K Phung, L Behbahani & J Allain, 'Governance gaps in eradicating forced labor: From global to domestic supply chains', *Regulation & Governance*, vol. 13, no. 1, 2017 pp. 1–21; D Weil, 'Creating a strategic enforcement approach to address wage theft: One academic's journey in organizational change', *Journal of Industrial Relations*, vol. 60, no. 3, 2018, pp. 437–60.

23 International Labour Organization, 'International Framework Agreements: A global tool for supporting rights at work International', 2007, <www.ilo.org/global/about-the-ilo/newsroom/news/WCMS_080723/lang--en/index.htm>; RM Locke & M Romis, 'The promise and perils of private voluntary regulation: Labor standards and work organization in two Mexican garment factories', *Review of International Political Economy*, vol. 17, no. 1, 2010, pp. 45–74.

24 J Ruggie, *Just Business: Multinational Corporations and Human Rights*, Norton Global Ethics Series, WW Norton & Company, New York, 2013.

25 T Clarke & M Boersma, 'The governance of global value chains: Unresolved human rights, environmental and ethical dilemmas in the Apple supply chain', *Journal of Business Ethics*, vol. 143, no. 1, 2015, pp. 111–31.

26 United States Department of Labor, 'List of goods produced by child labor or forced labor', 2018, <www.dol.gov/sites/default/files/documents/ilab/ListofGoods.pdf>.

27 International Labour Organization, 'Global estimates of modern slavery, forced labour and forced marriage', 2017, <www.ilo.org/global/publications/books/WCMS_575479/lang--en/index.htm>.

28 R Anker & M Anker, *Living Wages Around the World: Manual for Measurement*, Edward Elgar Publishing, Cheltenham, UK, 2017.

29 *Fair Work Ombudsman v Maroochy Sunshine Pty Ltd & Anor* [2017] FCCA 559, 2 ('Maroochy Sunshine Case').

30 Maroochy Sunshine Case (n 48), p. 47.

31 M Zirnsak et al, 'Submission to the inquiry into establishing a Modern Slavery Act', Joint standing committee on foreign affairs, defence and trade & sub-committee on reign affairs and aid, 2017, <endslavery.salvos.org.au/wp-content/uploads/2017/03/Sub-199.pdf>, p. 24.

32 Maroochy Sunshine Case (n 48).
33 Maroochy Sunshine Case (n 48), p. 56.
34 KnowTheChain, 'Food & beverage benchmark findings report', 2018, <knowthechain.org/wp-content/uploads/KTC_FB_2018.pdf>.
35 S Darlington, F Charner & M Castro, 'Thousands forced to work on Brazil's cattle ranches', CNN, 2017, <edition.cnn.com/2017/04/26/americas/brazil-amazon-slavery-freedom-project/index.html>.
36 Business & Human Rights Resource Centre, 'Attacked on defenders in the area of business and human rights', 2017, <www.business-humanrights.org/en/key-findings-from-the-database-of-attacks-on-human-rights-defenders-feb-2017>.
37 E Htusan, M Mason, R McDowell & M Mendoza, 'Associated Press explore: Seafood from slaves', *Associated Press*, 2016, <www.ap.org/explore/seafood-from-slaves/>.
38 Walk Free Foundation, 'Global slavery index: Country Data Thailand', 2018, <www.globalslaveryindex.org/2018/data/country-data/thailand/>.
39 K Hodal & CKF Lawrence, 'Revealed: Asian slave labour producing prawns for supermarkets in US, UK', *The Guardian*, 2014, <www.theguardian.com/global-development/2014/jun/10/supermarket-prawns-thailand-produced-slave-labour>.
40 Human Rights Watch, 'Thailand: Forced labor, trafficking persist in fishing fleets', 2018, <www.hrw.org/news/2018/01/23/thailand-forced-labor-trafficking-persist-fishing-fleets>.
41 A Kelly, 'Thai seafood: Are the prawns on your plate still fished by slaves?', *The Guardian*, 2018, <www.theguardian.com/global-development/2018/jan/23/thai-seafood-industry-report-trafficking-rights-abuses>.
42 A Murphy, 'Hidden chains: Rights abuses and forced labor in Thailand's fishing industry', Human Rights Watch, 2018, <www.hrw.org/sites/default/files/report_pdf/thailand0118_report_web.pdf>.
43 Kelly, 'Thai seafood', 2018.
44 Al Jazeera, 'Food chain slaves', *Slavery: A 21st Century Evil*, 2011, <www.aljazeera.com/programmes/slaverya21stcenturyevil/2011/10/201110108583163675.html>.
45 Ministry of Agriculture and Cooperatives, Department of Fisheries, Bangkok, *Marine Fisheries Management Plan of Thailand: A National Policy for Marine Fisheries Management, 2015–2019*, 2015, p. 10.
46 Human Rights Watch, 'Hidden chains: Rights abuses and forced

labour in Thailand's fishing industry', 2018, <www.hrw.org/sites/default/files/report_pdf/thailand0118_report_web.pdf>, pp. 15–16.
47 Human Rights Watch 2018.
48 UNIAP, 'Exploitation of Cambodian men at sea', 2009, <un-act.org/publication/view/siren-cb-03-exploitation-cambodian-men-sea/>, p. 5.
49 M Heller, 'Thai workers claim vindication in long battle with farm labor contractor', *Mint Press News*, 2014, <www.mintpressnews.com/thai-workers-claim-vindication-in-long-battle-with-farm-labor-contractor/187757/>.
50 W Culverwell, 'Farm labor contractor ordered to pay millions for mistreating Thai guest workers in Yakima Valley', *Tri-City Herald*, 2016, <www.tricityherald.com/news/business/agriculture/article74311757.html>.
51 United States Senate, 'Testimony of Meredith B. Stewart Southern Poverty Law Center before the Subcommittee on Immigration and the National Interest', 2016, <www.judiciary.senate.gov/download/06-08-16-stewart-testimony>.
52 C Felter, 'U.S. Temporary Foreign Worker Programs', *Council on Foreign Relations*, 2017, <www.cfr.org/backgrounder/us-temporary-foreign-worker-programs>.
53 Oxfam & IDEALS, 'A destiny of debts: Unmasking the prejudicial contracts in the Philippine banana industry', Make Fruit Fair, 2017 <makefruitfair.org/wp-content/uploads/2017/01/Destiny-of-Debts-Policy-Brief8_Final-1.pdf>.
54 D Dalabajan & AK Dinglasan, 'Land but no freedom: Debt, poverty and human suffering in the Philippine banana trade', Oxfam Library, 2018, <oxfamilibrary.openrepository.com/bitstream/handle/10546/620492/cs-land-but-no-freedom-philippine-bananas-210618-en.pdf?sequence=1>.
55 R Willoughby & T Gore, 'Ripe for change: Ending human suffering in supermarket supply chains', Oxfam, 2018, <oxfamilibrary.openrepository.com/bitstream/10546/620418/4/cr-ripe-for-change-supermarket-supply-chains-210618-en.pdf>.
56 Willoughby & Gore 2018.
57 A Abdulsamad & G Gereffi, Measurement in a world of globalized production, Duke Center on Globalization, Governance and Competitiveness, forthcoming.
58 D Vaughan-Whitehead & LP Caro, 'Purchasing practices and working conditions in global supply chains: Global Survey results (Fact sheet)', *International Labour Organization*, 2018, <www.ilo.

org/travail/info/fs/WCMS_556336/lang--en/index.htm>. For further discussion on Nike, see text at chapter 3, note 28.

59 International Labour Organization, 'Child labour in agriculture', <www.ilo.org/ipec/areas/Agriculture/lang--en/index.htm>.

60 International Labour Organization 2017.

61 L Taylor, 'Human vending machine dispenses "slave-made" food in UK', *Thomson Reuters Foundation*, 2018, < news.trust.org/item/20181210163940-dwy2a/>.

62 K Guilbert, 'Major companies urged to stop telling anti-slavery 'fairytales.", *Thomson Reuters Foundation*, 2018, <news.trust.org/item/20181104105401-ibglv/>.

63 G LeBaron, 'The global business of forced labour: Report of findings', *SPERI & University of Sheffield*, 2018, <globalbusinessofforcedlabour.ac.uk/wp-content/uploads/2018/05/Report-of-Findings-Global-Business-of-Forced-Labour.pdf>.

64 S Chaudhry & K Guilbert, 'Exclusive: Expose of labor abuse brews trouble for 'slave-free' India tea', *Reuters*, 2018, <www.reuters.com/article/us-india-forcedlabour-tea-idUSKCN1IW00H>.

65 L Nicholas, 'Cobalt supply chain needs transparency as human rights violations continue in DRC', *Small Caps*, 2018, <smallcaps.com.au/cobalt-supply-chain-transparency-human-rights-violations-drc/>.

66 T Wilson, 'In battery boom cobalt-supply chain, Democratic Republic of Congo has the power', *The Sydney Morning Herald*, 2017, <www.smh.com.au/business/in-battery-boom-cobaltsupply-chain-democratic-republic-of-congo-has-the-power-20171029-gzae9m.html>.

67 Afrewatch & Amnesty International, "This is what we die for: Human rights abuses in the Democratic Republic of the Congo power the global trade in cobalt', *Amnesty International*, 2016, <www.amnesty.org/download/Documents/AFR6231832016ENGLISH.PDF>.

68 Z Leslie, J Sarich & K Stauss, 'The Congo report: Slavery in Conflict Minerals', *Free the Slaves*, 2011, <www.freetheslaves.net/wp-content/uploads/2015/03/The-Congo-Report-English.pdf>; C Kennedy, 'Congo's mining slaves: Enslavement at South Kivu mining sites', *Free the Slaves*, 2013, <www.freetheslaves.net/wp-content/uploads/2015/03/Congos-Mining-Slaves-web-130622.pdf>.

69 T Frankel, 'This is where your smartphone battery begins', *Washington Post*, 2016, <www.washingtonpost.com/graphics/business/batteries/congo-cobalt-mining-for-lithium-ion-battery/>.

70 Afrewatch, & Amnesty International 2016.
71 A Lavoipierre, S Smiley & L Evelin, '"Worst possible form of child labour" to mine cobalt for phone batteries', *ABC*, 2018, <www.abc.net.au/news/2018-07-25/cobalt-child-labour-smartphone-batteries-congo/10031330>.
72 *Convention concerning the Prohibition and Immediate Action for the Elimination of the Worst Forms of Child Labour*, signed 17 June 1999, 2133 UNTS 161 (entered into force 29 November 2000).
73 Afrewatch, & Amnesty International 2016.
74 Afrewatch, & Amnesty International 2016.
75 Amnesty International, 'Time to recharge corporate action and inaction to tackle abuses in the cobalt supply chain', 2017, <www.amnesty.org/download/documents/afr6273952017english.pdf>.
76 C Cornish & H Sanderson, 'Amnesty warns on use of child labour in cobalt mining', *Financial Times*, 2017, <www.ft.com/content/bec64762-c923-11e7-ab18-7a9fb7d6163e>.
77 Responsible Business Alliance, 'About the Responsible Business Alliance', <www.responsiblebusiness.org/about/rba/>.
78 M Boersma, 'Between norms and practice: Civil society perspectives on the legitimacy of multistakeholder initiatives to eliminate child labor', *Business Strategy and the Environment*, vol. 27, no. 5, 2018, pp. 612–20.
79 P Lujala, SA Rustad & PL Billon, 'Has the EITI been successful? Reviewing evaluations of the Extractive Industries Transparency Initiative', Chr. Michelsen Institute, Bergen, 2017, <www.cmi.no/publications/6300-has-the-eiti-been-successful>.
80 I Kolstad & A Wiig, 'Is transparency the key to reducing corruption in resource-rich countries?', *World Development*, vol. 37, no. 3, 2009, pp. 521–32.
81 N Peyton, 'Electric car demand fuelling rise in child labour in DR Congo – campaigners', *Thomson Reuters Foundation*, 2018, <news.trust.org/item/20181102144515-pvelt/>.
82 R Bilton, M Bardo, J Oliver, A Head & C Thomas, 'Apple's broken promises', *BBC One*, 2014, <www.bbc.co.uk/programmes/b04vs348>.
83 A Callaway, 'Powering down corruption: Tackling transparency and human rights risks from Congo's cobalt mines to global supply chains', *Enough Project*, 2018, <enoughproject.org/wp-content/uploads/poweringdowncorruption_enough_oct2018-web.pdf>.
84 A Taylor, 'North Korea has 2.6 million "modern slaves" new report estimates', *Washington Post*, 2018, <www.washingtonpost.com/

news/worldviews/wp/2018/07/19/north-korea-has-2-6-million-modern-slaves-new-report-estimates/>.

85 S Borowiec, 'North Koreans perform $975 million worth of forced labor each year', *LA Times*, 2016, <www.latimes.com/world/asia/la-fg-north-korea-forced-labor-20161006-snap-story.html>.

86 R Perper & TF Chan, '1 in 10 North Koreans are forced into modern day slavery, human-rights study estimates', *Business Insiders*, 2018, <www.businessinsider.com.au/north-korea-modern-day-slavery-2018-7>.

87 United Nations Office of the High Commissioner of Human Rights, 'Sweatshop, North Korea', 2016, <tbinternet.ohchr.org/treaties/crc/shared%20documents/prk/int_crc_ngo_prk_26561_e.pdf>.

88 Human Rights Watch, 'North Korea: Forced labor underpins party congress', 2016, <www.hrw.org/news/2016/05/05/north-korea-forced-labor-underpins-party-congress>.

89 'Supply chains based on modern slavery may reach into the West', *The Economist*, 2018, <www.economist.com/graphic-detail/2018/07/19/supply-chains-based-on-modern-slavery-may-reach-into-the-west?fbclid=iwar0wxtx7muw_lqvrxk9w-efncbr6_hsswpk3zx4jr8mvntim1ukzhwyc6au>.

90 S Wong & P Wen, 'North Korea factories humming with "Made in China" clothes, traders say', *Reuters*, 2017, <www.reuters.com/article/us-northkorea-labour-china-insight-iduskbn1at00q>.

91 Wong & Wen 2017.

92 N McKenzie & R Baker, (2016, February 20). Surf clothing label Rip Curl using 'slave labour' to manufacture clothes in North Korea. Retrieved from www.smh.com.au/business/surf-clothing-label-rip-curl-using-slave-labour-to-manufacture-clothes-in-north-korea-20160220-gmz375.html

93 Wong & Wen 2017.

94 BBC, 'North Korea's secret slave gangs', 2018, <www.bbc.com/news/av/world-asia-43758908/north-korea-s-secret-slave-gangs>.

95 J McLaughlin, 'US cracks down on North Korea's army of overseas workers', CNN, 2018, <www.cnn.com/2018/06/25/politics/us-north-korea-overseas-workers/index.html>.

96 S Denyer & MJ Kim, 'South Korea envisions a building boom in the North. But Pyongyang still relies on "forced labor" brigades', *Washington Post*, 2018, <www.washingtonpost.com/world/asia_pacific/south-korea-envisions-a-building-boom-in-the-north-but-pyongyang-still-relies-on-forced-labor-

brigades/2018/12/16/687defaa-f2de-11e8-9240-e8028a62c722_story.html>.
97 'Forced labor in Uzbekistan's cotton fields was present in 2018 harvest', Cotton Campaign, 2019, <www.cottoncampaign.org/1/post/2019/01/forced-labor-in-uzbekistans-cotton-fields-was-present-in-2018-harvest.html>; 'Reports of forced labor in Turkmenistan's cotton sector', Cotton Campaign, <www.cottoncampaign.org/reports-of-forced-labor-in-turkmenistans-cotton-sector.html>.
98 Anti-Slavery International, 'Cotton Crimes: Uzbekistan and Turkmenistan', <www.antislavery.org/what-we-do/uzbekistan-turkmenistan/>.
99 S Malo, 'U.S. bans imports of slave-picked cotton from Turkmenistan', *Reuters*, 2018, <www.reuters.com/article/us-usa-trafficking-turkmenistan-iduskcn1ip3ub>.
100 Uzbek-German Forum for Human Rights, '"We want farmers to have full freedom": No need for forced labor when farmers are empowered to pay decent wages: spring cotton fieldwork 2018', 2018, <uzbekgermanforum.org/we-want-farmers-to-have-full-freedom-no-need-for-forced-labor-when-farmers-are-empowered-to-pay-decent-wages-spring-cotton-fieldwork-2018/>.
101 K Guilbert, 'Campaigners challenge U.N. over forced labor in Uzbekistan's cotton industry', *Reuters*, 2018, <www.reuters.com/article/us-uzbekistan-labour-workers-iduskcn1ns1s6>.
102 Human Rights Watch, '"We can't refuse to pick cotton": | Forced and child labor linked to World Bank Group Investments in Uzbekistan', 2017, <www.hrw.org/report/2017/06/27/we-cant-refuse-pick-cotton/forced-and-child-labor-linked-world-bank-group>.
103 Human Rights Watch, 'Uzbekistan: Forced labor linked to World Bank', 27 June 2017, <www.hrw.org/news/2017/06/27/uzbekistan-forced-labor-linked-world-bank>.
104 S Malo, 'Walmart looking into note found recounting forced labor in China', *Reuters*, 2017, <www.reuters.com/article/us-usa-trafficking-walmart-iduskbn1862zb>.
105 S Qiu & AM Roantree, 'Job jitters mount as China's factories sputter ahead of Lunar New Year', *Reuters*, 2019, <www.reuters.com/article/us-china-trade-labour-insight-iduskcn1pb2wo>.
106 Y Yang, 'Supply chains: the dirty secret of China's prisons', *Financial Times*, 2018, <www.ft.com/content/1416a056-833b-11e7-94e2-c5b903247afd>.
107 A France-Presse, 'Qantas, BA in China prison labour row', *New*

com.au, 2013, <www.news.com.au/travel/travel-updates/qantas-ba-in-china-prison-labour-row/news-story/1f54da5d22bdc12951ed5763c896875e>.

108 Y Yang 2018.

109 United States Customs and Border Protection, 'Detention orders (Withhold Release Orders) | U.S. Customs and Border Protection', <www.cbp.gov/trade/trade-community/programs-outreach/convict-importations/detention-orders>.

110 Institute for Criminal Policy Research, & Birkbeck University of London, 'Highest to lowest – prison population rate | world prison brief', *Prison Studies*, <www.prisonstudies.org/highest-to-lowest/prison_population_rate?field_region_taxonomy_tid=Al>.l>.

111 K Lexington, 'Prison labour is a billion-dollar industry, with uncertain returns for inmates', *The Economist*, 2017, <www.economist.com/united-states/2017/03/16/prison-labour-is-a-billion-dollar-industry-with-uncertain-returns-for-inmates>.

112 V Peláez, 'The prison industry in the United States: Big business or a new form of slavery?', *Global Research*, 2018, <www.globalresearch.ca/the-prison-industry-in-the-united-states-big-business-or-a-new-form-of-slavery/8289>.

113 D Moritz-Rabson, 'Inmates in government prisons are paid pennies to manufacture clothing, license plates and office supplies', *Newsweek*, 2018, <www.newsweek.com/prison-slavery-who-benefits-cheap-inmate-labor-1093729>.

114 C Schermerhorn, 'Prisoner strike exposes an age old American reliance on forced labor, *The Conversation*, 2018, <theconversation.com/prisoner-strike-exposes-an-age-old-american-reliance-on-forced-labor-102159>.

115 A Shahshahani, 'Why are for-profit US prisons subjecting detainees to forced labor?, *The Guardian*, 2018, <www.theguardian.com/commentisfree/2018/may/17/us-private-prisons-forced-labour-detainees-modern-slavery>.

116 PennState Law – Center for Immigrants' Rights Clinic, 'Imprisoned justice: Inside two Georgia immigrant detention centers', *Project South*, 2017, <projectsouth.org/wp-content/uploads/2017/06/Imprisoned_Justice_Report-1.pdf>.

117 P Chamberlain & R Cookson, 'The prisoners providing cheap labour for public services', *The Guardian*, 2010, <www.theguardian.com/society/2010/oct/05/prisoners-cheap-labour-public-services>.

118 Organisation for Economic Co-operation and Development, 'Size of public procurement', *Government at a Glance*, 2017, <doi.

org/10.1787/gov_glance-2017-59-en>.

119 M Boersma, 'Do no harm? Procurement of medical goods by Australian companies and government', Australian Nursing and Midwifery Federation & The Australia Institute, 2017, <www.anmf.org.au/documents/Do_No_Harm_Report.pdf>.

120 M Bhutta & A Santhakumar, 'In good hands', British Medical Association, Medical Fair and Ethical Trade Group, European Working Group on Ethical Public Procurement', 2016, <https://www.bma.org.uk/collective-voice/influence/international/global-justice/fair-medical-trade/ethical-procurement-issues>; K Adams, 'Nowhere to turn: Addressing Australian corporate abuses overseas', Human Rights Law Centre, 2018, <static1.squarespace.com/static/580025f66b8f5b2dabbe4291/t/5c1aa50a8a922db8f09e5c1b/1545250097352/Nowhere+to+Turn.pdf>.

121 N Khadem, 'Locked-up passports, crowded living: Ansell glove supplier accused of abusing workers' rights', ABC, 2018, <www.abc.net.au/news/2018-12-08/rubber-gloves-supplier-to-ansell-accused-abusing-worker-rights/10595996>.

122 L Tickle, 'Why does so much of the NHS's surgical equipment start life in the sweatshops of Pakistan?', *The Independent*, 2015, <www.independent.co.uk/life-style/health-and-families/features/why-does-so-much-of-the-nhss-surgical-equipment-start-life-in-the-sweatshops-of-pakistan-9988885.html>.

123 Swedwatch, 'The dark side of healthcare', Vimeo, 2007, <vimeo.com/48130343>.

124 United States Department of Labor, 'List of goods produced by child labor or forced labor', 2018, <www.dol.gov/sites/default/files/documents/ilab/listofgoods.pdf>.

Chapter 3—Emergence of the corporate social conscience?

1 M Muller 'Nestlé baby milk scandal has grown up but not gone away', *The Guardian,* 2013 < https://www.theguardian.com/sustainable-business/nestle-baby-milk-scandal-food-industry-standards>.

2 J Richter, *Holding Corporations Accountable: Corporate Conduct, International Codes and Citizen Action*, Zed Books, London, 2001.

3 M McGrath, 'World's largest food and beverage companies 2018: Anheuser-Busch, Nestle and Pepsi top the list', *Forbes*, 2018, <www.forbes.com/sites/maggiemcgrath/2018/06/06/worlds-largest-food-and-beverage-companies-2018-anheuser-busch-nestle-and-pepsi-top-the-list/#e15e57b1b08d>.

4 *Doe v. Nestle* No. 17-55435 (9th Cir, 2018).
5 Verité, 'Recruitment practices and migrant labor conditions in Nestlé's Thai shrimp supply chain: An examination of forced labor and other human rights risks endemic to the Thai seafood sector', 2015, <www.verite.org/wp-content/uploads/2016/11/NestleReport-ThaiShrimp_prepared-by-Verite.pdf>.
6 Nestlé, 'Nestlé in society: Creating Shared Value and meeting our commitments 2017', 2017,<www.nestle.com/asset-library/documents/library/documents/corporate_social_responsibility/nestle-in-society-summary-report-2017-en.pdf>, p. 5. Not all agree with the utility of shared value. For a critique of the concept see, A Crane, G Palazzo, LJ Spence & D Matten, 'Contesting the value of creating shared value', *California Management Review*, vol. 56, no. 2, 2014, pp. 130–54.
7 Fortune 500, 'Fortune 500 List', <fortune.com/fortune500/>.
8 World Bank Group, *A Measured Approach to Ending Poverty and Boosting Shared Prosperity: Concepts, Data, and the Twin Goals*, 2015; The Economist, 'Towards the end of poverty', 2013, <www.economist.com/leaders/2013/06/01/towards-the-end-of-poverty>.
9 Business & Human Rights Resource Centre, 'Walmart lawsuit (re gender discrimination in USA)', <www.business-humanrights.org/en/walmart-lawsuit-re-gender-discrimination-in-usa>.
10 B Stephens, 'The amorality of profit: Transnational corporations and human rights', *Berkeley Journal of International Law*, vol. 20, no. 1, 2002, pp. 44–90, 45. For a wealth of information on the all aspects of corporate interaction on human rights issues, see Business & Human Rights Resource Centre, <www.business-humanrights.org/>.
11 Asia Floor Wage Alliance, 'Precarious work in the Walmart global value chain', *International Trade Union Confederation*, 2016, <www.ituc-csi.org/IMG/pdf/afwa_walmart.pdf>.
12 M Friedman, 'The social responsibility of business is to increase its profits', *New York Times*, 1970, <www.nytimes.com/1970/09/13/archives/article-15-no-title.html>.
13 P Whiteford, 'The "inequality wars": CEO pay is one part of a complex picture post-GFC', *ABC News*, 2017, <www.abc.net.au/news/2017-12-07/ceo-pay-better-than-pre-gfc-rising-inequality/9234634>.
14 Friedman 1970.
15 Sproutsocial, 'Championing change in the age of social media', 2017, <sproutsocial.com/insights/data/

championing-change-in-the-age-of-social-media/?utm_source=newsletter&utm_medium=email&utm_campaign=sendto_newslettertest&stream=top-stories#About-the-Data>.

16 Edelman, 'Edelman Trust Barometer', 2019, <www.edelman.com/trust-barometer>.

17 Global Labor Justice, 'Gender based violence in the H&M garment supply chain: A report to the ILO 2018', 2018, pp. 4, 24, <www.globallaborjustice.org/wp-content/uploads/2018/05/GBV-HM-May-2018.pdf>.

18 A Kashyap, 'Work faster or get out: Labour rights abuses in Cambodia's garment industry', *Human Rights Watch*, 2015, <www.hrw.org/report/2015/03/11/work-faster-or-get-out/labor-rights-abuses-cambodias-garment-industry>.

19 World Bank, 'In Bangladesh, empowering and employing women in the garments sector', 2017, <www.worldbank.org/en/news/feature/2017/02/07/in-bangladesh-empowering-and-employing-women-in-the-garments-sector>.

20 World Bank 2017, p. 34.

21 Deloitte, 'The 2016 Deloitte millennial survey: Winning over the next generation of leaders', 2016, <www2.deloitte.com/content/dam/Deloitte/global/Documents/About-Deloitte/gx-millenial-survey-2016-exec-summary.pdf>.

22 The difference between what consumers say and what their purchasing practices reflect is discussed in chapter 5.

23 United Nations, *Global Compact*, <www.unglobalcompact.org/what-is-gc/participants>.

24 Human Rights Council, *Guiding Principles on Business and Human Rights: Implementing the United Nations 'Protect, Respect and Remedy' Framework', Report of the Special Representative of the Secretary-General on the issue of Human Rights and Transnational Corporations and Other Business Enterprises*, UN Doc A/HRC/17/31, 21 March 2011.

25 For example, see the International Labour Organization, 'Tripartite declaration of principles concerning multinational enterprises and social policy', 2017, <www.ilo.org/empent/Publications/WCMS_094386/lang--en/index.htm>.

26 LC Backer , 'Rights and Accountability in Development ('RAID') v DAS Air and Global Witness v Afrimex: Small steps towards an autonomous transnational legal system for the regulation of multinational corporations', *Melbourne Journal of International Law*, vol.10, no.1, 2009, pp. 258–307, 258; K Genovese, 'Access to

remedy: Non-judicial grievance mechanisms', Business & Human Rights Resource Centre, <www.business-humanrights.org/en/access-to-remedy-through-non-judicial-grievance-mechanisms>.

27 Human Rights Law Centre, 'Nowhere to turn: Addressing Australian corporate abuse overseas', 2018, < www.hrlc.org.au/reports/nowhere-to-turn>, p. 14.

28 Nike, 'Frequently asked questions', <nikeinc.com/pages/frequently-asked-questions>.

29 D O'Rourke, 'Smoke from a hired gun: A critique of Nike's labor and environmental auditing in Vietnam as performed by Ernst & Young', *San Francisco Transnational Resource and Action Center*, 1997, <nature.berkeley.edu/orourke/PDF/smoke.pdf>, p. 6. Although this quote references Nike as 'employing' some 350 000 workers, the workers were not employed directly by Nike but rather were employed by the company operating the factory in which the garments were produced. See also the reproduction of the leaked Ernst &Young Environmental and Labor Practice Audit report of 13 January 1997: Corpwatch, 'Ernst & Young environmental and labor practice audit of the Tae Kwang Vina Industrial Ltd Co, Vietnam', 1997, <www.corpwatch.org/article.php?id=2488>

30 M Nisen, 'Why the Bangladesh factory collapse would never have happened to Nike', *Business Insider Australia*, 2013, <www.businessinsider.com/how-nike-solved-its-sweatshop-problem-2013-5>.

31 Nike, 'Sustainability', <about.nike.com/pages/sustainability>.

32 M Boersma, 'Between norms and practice: Civil society perspectives on the legitimacy of multistakeholder initiatives to eliminate child labor', *Business Strategy and the Environment*, vol. 27, no. 5, 2018, pp.612–20.

33 Human Rights Watch, 'UN Human Rights Council: Weak stance on business standards', 2011, <www.hrw.org/news/2011/06/16/un-human-rights-council-weak-stance-business-standards>.

34 M Boersma 'Changing approaches to child labour in global supply chains: Exploring the influence of multi-stakeholder partnerships and the United Nations Guiding Principles on Business and Human Rights', *UNSW Law Journal*, vol. 40, no. 3, 2017, pp. 1249–72.

35 Human Rights Council, *Elaboration of an Internationally Legally Binding Instrument on Transnational Corporations and other Business Enterprises with Respect to Human Rights*, UN Doc. A/HRC/26/L.22/Rev.1, 25 June 2014.

36 J Ruggie, 'Quo vadis? Unsolicited advice to business and human rights treaty sponsors', *Institute for Human Rights and Business*, 2014, <www.ihrb.org/commentary/quo-vadis-unsolicited-advice-business.html>. For broad commentary on the potential treaty, see <business-humanrights.org/en/binding-treaty>.

37 *Mankayi v AngloGold Ashanti Ltd* [2011] (CCT 40/10) ZACC 3. See summary at Business & Human Rights Resource Centre, 'AngloGold Ashanti silicosis lawsuit (So. Africa)', <www.business-humanrights.org/en/anglogold-ashanti-silicosis-lawsuit-so-africa>.

38 Business & Human Rights Resource Centre, 'Yahoo! Lawsuit (re China)', <www.business-humanrights.org/en/yahoo-lawsuit-re-china-0>.

39 J Boudreau, 'Lawmaker scolds Yahoo: "Morally you are pygmies"', *The Mercury News*, 2007, <www.mercurynews.com/2007/11/06/lawmaker-scolds-yahoo-morally-you-are-pygmies/>.

40 Human Rights Law Centre 2018, p. 12.

41 D Bilchitz & S Deva, *The Human Rights Obligations of Business: Beyond the Corporate Responsibility to Respect*, Cambridge University Press, Cambridge, 2013, p. 2.

42 The Economist Intelligence Unit, 'The road from principles to practices: Today's challenged for business in respecting human rights', *Universal Rights Group Geneva*, 2016, < www.universal-rights.org/urg-policy-reports/the-road-from-principles-to-practice-todays-challenges-for-business-in-respecting-human-rights/>, p. 4.

43 The Economist Intelligence Unit 2016, p. 5.

44 A Taylor, 'Bhopal: The world's worst industrial disaster, 30 years later', *The Atlantic*, 2014, <www.theatlantic.com/photo/2014/12/bhopal-the-worlds-worst-industrial-disaster-30-years-later/100864/>.

45 S Labowitz & D Baumann-Pauly, 'Business as usual is not an option: Supply chains and sourcing after Rana Plaza', *NYU Stern*, 2014, <www.stern.nyu.edu/cons/groups/content/documents/webasset/con_047408.pdf>, p. 14.

46 Media reports estimate there may be between 5000 and 6000 factories in Bangladesh, but the exact number remains unclear. See, for example, J Burke, 'Bangladesh factory fires: Fashion industry's latest crisis', *The Guardian*, 2013, <www.theguardian.com/world/2013/dec/08/bangladesh-factory-fires-fashion-latest-crisis>.

47 Labowitz & Baumann-Pauly 2014, p. 16.

48 R Smithers, 'Benetton admits link with firm in collapsed

Bangladesh building', *The Guardian*, 2013, <www.theguardian.com/world/2013/apr/29/benetton-link-collapsed-building-bangladesh>.

49 Labor Exploitation Advisory Group, 'Labor compliance to exploitation and the abuses in-between', 2016, <www.laborexploitation.org/publications/labor-exploitation-advisory-group-leag-position-paper-labor-compliance-exploitation>; K Skrivankova, 'Between decent work and forced labor: Examining the continuum of exploitation', Gangmasters & Labour Abuse Authority, 2010, <www.gla.gov.uk/media/1585/jrf-between-decent-work-and-forced-labor.pdf>; Ethical Trade Initiative, 'Managing risks associated with modern slavery: A good practice note for the private sector', 2018, <www.ethicaltrade.org/sites/default/files/shared_resources/Managing%20risks%20associated%20with%20modern%20slavery.pdf>.

50 G Lebaron, 'The global business of forced labour', University of Sheffield, 2018, <globalbusinessofforcedlabour.ac.uk/wp-content/uploads/2018/05/Report-of-Findings-Global-Business-of-Forced-Labour.pdf>.

51 Ranking Digital Rights, 'Corporate accountability', 2017, <rankingdigitalrights.org/index2017/assets/static/download/RDRindex2017report.pdf>. In 2017 Google announced it had surpassed two billion active monthly users: L Matney, 'Google has 2 billion users on Andriod and 500M on Google Photos', *Tech Crunch*, 2017, <techcrunch.com/2017/05/17/google-has-2-billion-users-on-android-500m-on-google-photos/>. For the Baidu estimate, see A Boxall, 'Baidu ad platform has 800 million monthly active users, sees 50% annual increase in developer support', *Business of Apps*, 2017, <www.businessofapps.com/baidu-ad-platform-has-800-million-monthly-active-users-sees-50-annual-increase-in-developer-support/>.

52 E Bagshaw, 'The Australian companies mining $40 billion out of Africa', *Sydney Morning Herald*, 2017, <www.smh.com.au/politics/federal/the-australian-companies-mining-40-billion-out-of-africa-20170906-gyc6t0.html>.

53 W Fitzgibbon, MM Hamilton & CS Gallego, 'Australian mining companies digging a deadly footprint in Africa', *International Consortium of Investigative Journalists*, 2015, <www.icij.org/investigations/fatal-extraction/australian-mining-companies-digging-deadly-footprint-africa/>.

54 DM Mayer, M Ong, S Sonenshein & SJ Ashford, 'The money or the morals? When moral language is more effective for

selling social issues', *Journal of Applied Psychology*, 2019, <dx.doi.org/10.1037/apl0000388>.

55 K Ryssdal, 'Unilever CEO: For Sustainable business, go against "mindless consumption"', Marketplace, 2013, quoted in DB Pauly & J Nolan, *Business and Human Rights: From Principles to Practice*, Routledge UK, 2016, p. 17.

56 M Posner, 'Making the business case for human rights: an assessment', NYU Stern, 2015, <bhr.stern.nyu.edu/blogs/2018/12/22/making-the-business-case-for-human-rights>, quoted in Pauly & Nolan, 2016, p. 14.

57 R Davis & DM Franks, 'Costs of company-community conflict in the extractive sector', Harvard Kennedy School CSR Initiative, 2014, <www.csrm.uq.edu.au/publications/costs-of-company-community-conflict-in-the-extractive-sector>.

58 'Host country' refers to the country in which a multinational company is operating (such as sourcing or manufacturing its products) and 'home country' refers to the home or place of incorporation of the multinational company.

Chapter 4—Regulating the business of modern slavery

1 The website slaveryfootprint.org allows consumers to visualise how their consumption habits are connected to modern-day slavery.

2 World Vision Australia, 'Chocolate's bitter taste: Forced, child and trafficked labour in the cocoa industry', 2015 <campaign.worldvision.com.au/wp-content/uploads/2015/03/7590_Easter_2015_Factsheet_Cocoa_WEB.pdf>, p. 1.

3 L Berg & B Farbenblum, 'Wage theft in Australia: Findings of the National Temporary Migrant Work Survey', *Analysis & Policy Observatory*, 2017, <apo.org.au/system/files/120406/apo-nid120406-483146.pdf>.

4 Agence France-Presse, 'Apple under fire again for working conditions at Chinese factories', *The Guardian*, 2014 <www.theguardian.com/technology/2014/dec/19/apple-under-fire-again-for-working-conditions-at-chinese-factories?CMP=EMCNEWEML6619I2>; C Duhigg & D Barboza, 'In China, human costs are built into an iPad', *New York Times*, 2012, <www.nytimes.com/2012/01/26/business/ieconomy-apples-ipad-and-the-human-costs-for-workers-in-china.html>; China Labor Watch, 'Beyond Foxconn: Deplorable working conditions characterize Apple's entire supply chain', *China Labor Watch*, 2012, <www.chinalaborwatch.org/

upfile/2012_8_13/2012627-5.pdf>; R Litzinger, 'Labor in China: A new politics of struggle', *South Atlantic Quarterly*, vol. 112, no. 1, 2013, pp. 172–8.

5 Duhigg & Barboza 2012.

6 A Chakrabortty, 'The woman who nearly died making your iPad', *The Guardian*, 2013, <www.theguardian.com/commentisfree/2013/aug/05/woman-nearly-died-making-ipad>.

7 Apple, 'Supplier Responsibility 2019 Progress Report', *Apple*, 2019, <www.apple.com/supplier-responsibility/pdf/Apple_SR_2019_Progress_Report.pdf>, p. 25.

8 P Utting, 'Rethinking business regulation: From self-control to social control', Research paper No. 15, United Nations Research Institute for Social Development, Technology, Business and Society, 2005, <www.unrisd.org/unrisd/website/document.nsf/462fc27bd1fce00880256b4a0060d2af/f02ac3db0ed406e0c12570a10029bec8/$FILE/utting.pdf>, p. 1.

9 A Ganesan, 'UN human rights council: Weak stance on business standards', Human Rights Watch, 16 June 2011, <www.hrw.org/news/2011/06/16/un-human-rights-council-weak-stance-business-standards>; AFLCIO, *Responsibility Outsourced: Social Audits, Workplace Certification and Twenty Years of Failure to Protect Worker Rights*, April 23, 2013, <www.aflcio.org/Learn-About-Unions/International-Labor-Movement/Responsibility-Outsourced-Report>.

10 RB Reich, *Supercapitalism: The Transformation of Business, Democracy and Everyday Life*, Alfred A Knopf, New York, 2007, p. 170.

11 A D'Amato, 'Softness in international law: A self-serving quest for new legal materials: A reply to Jean d'Aspremont', *European Journal of International Law*, vol. 20, no. 3, 2009, pp. 897–910.

12 C Oka, 'Accounting for the gaps in labour standard compliance: The role of reputation-conscious buyers in the Cambodian garment industry', *European Journal of Development Research*, vol. 22, no. I, 2010, pp. 59–78.

13 *Tariff Act of 1930*, 19 USC § 1654 (US); *Federal Acquisitions Regulation (FAR)* 48 CFR 1, 22.17 (US), *Child Labour Due Diligence Law 2017* (Netherlands); *Modern Slavery Act 2015* (UK), s 54; *Duty of Vigilance Law 2017* (France); *Dodd-Frank Wall Street Reform and Consumer Protection Act* 12 USC § 1502 ('Dodd-Frank Act'); *Transparency in Supply Chains Act of 2010*, Cal Civil Code §1714.43; *Conflict Minerals Regulation 2021* (EU), *Responsible Business Initiative* (Switzerland), *Modern Slavery Act 2018* (Cth); *Modern Slavery Act 2018* (NSW).

14 *Transparency in Supply Chains Act of 2010*, Cal Civil Code Section 1714.43.
15 United States of America Department of State, Trafficking in Persons Report, July 2015, pp. 330–4.
16 Monica *Sud v. Costco Wholesale Corporation, et al* No. 4:2015-cv03783 - Document 93 (N.D. Cal. 2017), p. 3.
17 *Hodson v. Mars, Inc* No. 16-15444, D.C. No. 3:15-cv-04450 RS (N.D. Cal. 2018), *p. 4.*
18 UK Home Office, *Modern Slavery and Supply Chains Consultation*, 2015, p. 15.
19 UK Government, *UK Annual Report on Modern Slavery*, 2017.
20 *Galdikas & Ors v. DJ Houghton Catching Services Ltd & Ors* [2016] EWHC 1376 (QB) ('*Goldikas v. DJ Houghton*').
21 Leigh Day, 'Judgment against "UK's worst gangmaster" in favour of modern slavery victims', 2016, <www.leighday.co.uk/News/News-2016/June-2016/Judgment-against-UKs-Worst-Gangmaster-in-favour>.
22 *Galdikas v. DJ Houghton* (n 18) [42].
23 Galdikas v DJ Houghton et al [2016] EWHC 1376 (QB)
24 Nerijus Antuzis and others v DJ Houghton et al [2019] EWHC 843 (QB)
25 Anti-Slavery International, 'Trafficking for forced labour: UK Country report', 2006, <www.antislavery.org/wpcontent/uploads/2017/01/trafficking_for_forced_labour_uk_country_report-1.pdf>, p. 26.
26 A Ionova, 'Is landmark UK law falling short in fight against modern slavery?', *Thomson Reuters*, 2018, <www.reuters.com/article/us-britain-slavery-law/is-landmark-uk-law-falling-short-in-fight-against-modern-slavery-idUSKBN1GV07V>.
27 C Bayer & J Hudson, *Corporate Compliance with the California Transparency in Supply Chains Act: Anti-Slavery Performance in 2016*, March 2017, p. 5.
28 R Birkey, R Guidrey, MA Islam & D Patten, 'Mandated social disclosure: An analysis of the response to the California Transparency in Supply Chains Act 2010', *Journal of Business Ethics*, vol. 152, no. 3, 2018, pp. 827–41, <link.springer.com/article/10.1007%2Fs10551-016-3364-7>.
29 T Benjamin & JG Purvis, 'Corporate supply chain transparency: California's seminal attempt to discourage forced labour', *International Journal of Human Rights*, vol. 20 no. 1, 2016, pp. 55–77; Ergon Associates, *Reporting on Modern Slavery:*

The Current State of Disclosure, May 2016; Core Coalition & Business & Human Rights Resource Centre, 'Register of slavery & human trafficking corporate statements released to date to comply with the UK Modern Slavery Act 2016', Modern Slavery Registry, <www.modernslaveryregistry.org/>; Know the Chain, 'Five years of the California Transparency in Supply Chains Act', 2015, <knowthechain.org/wp-content/uploads/2015/10/KnowTheChain_InsightsBrief_093015.pdf>.

30 S George, 'British retailers call for progress on "weak" corporate anti-slavery commitments', Edie.Net, 2018, < www.edie.net/news/7/M-S--Tesco-and-Co-op-call-for-unification-of-business--anti-slavery-commitments--/>.

31 M Bloomfield & G LeBaron, 'The UK Modern Slavery Act: Transparency through disclosure in global governance', *E-International News*, 2018, <www.e-ir.info/2018/09/21/the-uk-modern-slavery-act-transparency-through-disclosure-in-global-governance/>.

32 M Carrigan & A Attalla, 'The myth of the ethical consumer: Do ethics matter in purchase behaviour?', *Journal of Consumer Marketing*, vol.18, no. 7, 2001, pp. 560–77.

33 F Field, M Miller & B Butler-Sloss, Home Office (UK), *Independent Review of the Modern Slavery Act*, Second interim report: Transparency in supply chains, January 2019, para. 2.5.2 ('UK Home Office January 2019 Independent Review').

34 Nestlé Australia, Submission No 76 to Senate Standing Committee on Legal and Constitutional Affairs, *Inquiry into a Modern Slavery Bill.*

35 Joint Standing Committee on Foreign Affairs, Defence and Trade, Parliament of the Commonwealth of Australia, *Hidden in Plain Sight*, December 2017; Senate Standing Committees on Legal and Constitutional Affairs, Parliament of the Commonwealth of Australia, *Report Modern Slavery Bill 2018 [Provisions]*, 24 August 2018.

36 Woolworths Group, Submission No 47 to Senate Legal and Constitutional Affairs Legislation Committee, *Inquiry* into Establishing a Modern Slavery Act in Australia, 28 July 2017, p. 2.

37 A Forrest, 'I found slaves in our supply chain', *Sydney Morning Herald*, 2018, <www.smh.com.au/national/i-found-slaves-in-our-supply-chain-20180701-p4zow9.html>.

38 NSW Farmers Submission No 191 to Joint Standing Committee on Foreign Affairs, Defence and Trade, Inquiry into a 'Modern

Slavery Act' for Australia, June 2017, p. 2.

39 Australian Government, Department of Home Affairs, *Modern Slavery Supply Chains Reporting Requirement Public Consultation Paper*, 2017, p. 3.

40 *LAW No 2017-399 of March 27, 2017 on the Duty of Vigilance of Parent Companies and Instructing Companies*, JORF No 0074 of 28 March 2017, text No. 1.

41 Sherpa, *Vigilance Plans Reference Guidance*, 2019, <www.asso-sherpa.org/wp-content/uploads/2019/02/Sherpa_VPRG_EN_WEB-ilovepdf-compressed.pdf>, p. 10.

42 As at June 2019 the Dutch Government had not yet stated when the implementation of the law will begin.

43 Dutch Agreement on Sustainable Garment and Textile (2016) <http://www.indianet.nl/pdf/AgreementOnSustainableGarmentAndTextile.pdf> and the Dutch Banking Sector Agreement on International Responsible Business Conduct Regarding Human Rights (October 2016), <https://www.imvoconvenanten.nl/banking?sc_lang=en>

44 Global Witness, 'The Dodd Frank Act's Section 1502 on conflict minerals', 2011, <www.globalwitness.org/en/archive/dodd-frank-acts-section-1502-conflict-minerals/>.

45 Dodd-Frank Act (n 13) § 1502. However, a 2019 report by the Danish Institute for International Studies and the International Peace Information Service argued that even though some armed groups rely on minerals for funding, they do not fuel conflict and that the responsible sourcing laws are having a negative impact on artisanal mining. K Matthysen, S Spittaels & P Schouten 'Mapping artisanal mining areas and mineral supply chains in eastern DR Congo Impact of armed interference & responsible sourcing', April 2019 <ipisresearch.be/wp-content/uploads/2019/04/1904-IOM-mapping-eastern-DRC.pdf>.

46 G Sarfaty, 'Shining light on global supply chains', *Harvard International Law Journal*, vol. 56, no. 2, 2015, pp. 419–63.

47 Greenpeace International, 'Taiwanese seafood giant linked to human rights violation', 2018, <www.greenpeace.org/international/press-release/16676/taiwanese-seafood-giant-linked-to-human-rights-violations-greenpeace/>.

48 A Sinclair & J Nolan, 'The Australian *Modern Slavery Act 2018*: Will it live up to expectations?', Business & Human Rights Resource Centre, 2018, <www. business-humanrights.org/en/the-australian-modern-slavery-act-2018-—will-it-live-up-to-expectations>.

49 LD Brandeis, *Other People's Money – and How Bankers Use It*, Frederick A. Stokes Company New York, 1914, p. 92.

50 As of August 2018, the Modern Slavery Registry contained 5620 statements of the estimated 12 000 required. A Phillips & A Trautrims, *Agriculture and Modern Slavery Act Reporting: Poor Performance Despite High Risks*, Office of the Independent Anti-Slavery Commissioner and the University of Nottingham's Rights Lab, 2018, <www.researchgate.net/publication/327060615_Agriculture_and_Modern_Slavery_Act_Reporting_Poor_Performance_Despite_High_Risks>.

51 I Ayres & J Braithwaite, *Responsive Regulation*, Oxford University Press, NewYork, 1992, chapter 2.

52 *Royal Commission into Misconduct in the Banking, Superannuation and Financial Services Industry*, 1 February 2019, vol. 1, p. 3.

53 Walk Free, 'The Global Slavery Index 2018', <www.globalslaveryindex.org/2018/findings/global-findings/>.

54 S Deva, 'Slavery and gender-blind regulatory responses', *Cambridge Core Blog*, 2019, <blog.journals.cambridge.org/2019/03/08/slavery-and-gender-blind-regulatory-responses/>.

55 United States Government Accountability Office, 'K–12 education: Better use of information could help agencies identify disparities and address racial discrimination', 2016, <assets.documentcloud.org/documents/2838279/GAO-Segregation-Report.pdf>.

56 Black Lives Matter, 'Herstory', <blacklivesmatter.com/about/herstory/>.

57 N Bose, 'Insight: Bangladesh struggles to check garment factories are safe', *Thomson Reuters*, 2013, <www.reuters.com/article/us-bangladesh-building-inspections-insig/insight-bangladesh-struggles-to-check-garment-factories-are-safe-idUSBRE96R0DA20130728>.

58 E Kenway, 'FLEX welcomes recommendations to give Modern Slavery Act "transparency" requirement more teeth', *Labour Exploitation*, 2019, <labourexploitation.org/news/flex-welcomes-recommendations-give-modern-slavery-act-transparency-requirement-more-teeth>.

59 *UK Home Office January 2019 Independent Review* (n 29) para. 2.3.1.

60 US State Department, *Trafficking in Persons*, June 2018, <www.state.gov/j/tip/rls/tiprpt/index.htm>, p. 43.

61 J Reinecke, J Donaghey, N Bocken & L Luriano 'Business models and labour standards: Making the connection', *Ethical Trading*

Initiative, 2019, <www.ethicaltrade.org/sites/default/files/shared_resources/Business%20models%20%26%20labour%20standards.pdf>, p. 3.

62 Oxfam, 'Trading away our rights: Women working in global supply chains', 2004, <www.oxfam.org/sites/www.oxfam.org/files/rights.pdf>, pp. 32–8.

63 J Davis-Peccoud & S Duchnowski, 'Snap chart: When sustainability requires dramatic change', *Bain & Company*, 2018, <www.bain.com/insights/when-sustainability-requires-dramatic-change-snap-chart/>.

64 Richard M Locke, The Promise and limits of Private Power: Promoting Labor Standards in a Global Economy, Cambridge University Press, New York, 2013, pp. 3–7.

65 International Labour Organization, 'INWORK issue Brief No. 10 Purchasing practices and working conditions in global supply chains: Global Survey results', June 2017, p. 7.

66 International Labour Organization 2017 p. 7.

67 M Boersma, 'Exploring legitimacy and exposing legitimising myths: A critical analysis of corporate social responsibility in global supply chains', PhD thesis, University of Technology, Sydney, 2019.

68 N Monebhurrun 'Consumer social responsibility as a requirement for corporate social responsibility', *Brazilian Journal of International Law*, vol 15, no. 2, 2018, pp. 13–17.

69 ICAR & Focus on Labour Exploitation, 'Full disclosure: Towards better modern slavery reporting', March 2019, p. 25.

70 Australian Human Rights Commission & EY, *Human Rights in Investment*, April 2017, <www.humanrights.gov.au/sites/default/files/document/publication/AHRC_EY_Investment%20and%20human%20rights%20Report%20April%202017.pdf>, p. 3.

71 M Kramer 'The backlash to Larry Fink's letter shows how far business has to go on social responsibility', *Harvard Business Review,* 2019, <hbr.org/2019/01/the-backlash-to-larry-finks-letter-shows-how-far-business-has-to-go-on-social-responsibility>.

72 C Gasparino & L Moynihan, 'BlackRock's Larry Fink rattles employees amid political posturing', *Fox Business*, 2019, <www.foxbusiness.com/business-leaders/blackrocks-larry-fink-rattles-employees-amid-political-posturing>.

73 KPMG, *The Road Ahead: The KPMG Survey of Corporate Responsibility Reporting*, 2017. These companies are the world's 250 largest companies by revenue based on the Fortune 500 ranking of 2016.

74 D Kovick & R Davis 'Tackling modern slavery and human trafficking at scale through financial sector leverage', *Shift Project*, 2019, <www.shiftproject.org/resources/collaborations/tackling-modern-slavery-and-human-trafficking-at-scale-through-financial-sector-leverage/>.

75 B Farbenblum, L Berg & A Kintominas, 'Transformative technology for migrant workers', *Open Society Foundation*, 2018, <www.opensocietyfoundations.org/reports/transformative-technology-migrant-workers-opportunities-challenges-and-risks>.

76 Fair Food Standards Council, 'Participating buyers', <www.fairfoodstandards.org/resources/participating-buyers/>.

77 Fair Food Standards Council, 'Fair Food Code of Conduct', <www.fairfoodstandards.org/resources/fair-food-code-of-conduct/>, part I, art. 5.

Chapter 5—Frontiers in the fight against modern slavery

1 Human Rights First, 'Human Trafficking by the Numbers', *Human Rights First*, 2017, <www.humanrightsfirst.org/resource/human-trafficking-numbers>

2 The Human Trafficking Legal Centre & WilmerHale, 'United States Federal Courts' continuing failure to order mandatory criminal restitution for human trafficking victims', September 2018, <www.htlegalcenter.org/wp-content/uploads/2018-Mandatory-Restitution-Report.pdf>.

3 J Fields, 'US ban on slave-made goods nets tiny fraction of $400 bln threat', *Thomson Reuters Foundation News*, 2019, <news.trust.org/item/20190408044809-3ud9e/>.

4 Organisation for Economic Co-operation and Development, OECD Due Diligence Guidance for Responsible Supply Chains of Minerals from Conflict-Affected and High-Risk Areas, OECD Publishing, Paris, 2016, <dx.doi.org/10.1787/9789264252479-en>; Organisation for Economic Co-operation and Development, 'OECD due diligence guidance for responsible supply chains in the garment and footwear sector', 2017, <www.oecd-ilibrary.org/governance/oecd-due-diligence-guidance-for-responsible-supply-chains-in-the-garment-and-footwear-sector_9789264290587-en>; Organisation for Economic Co-operation and Development & Food and Agriculture Organization of the United Nations, OECD-FAO Guidance for Responsible Agricultural Supply Chains, OECD Publishing, Paris, 2016, <dx.doi.org/10.1787/9789264251052-en>; Organisation for Economic

Co-operation and Development, 'Responsible business conduct for institutional investors: Key considerations for due diligence under the OECD Guidelines for Multinational Enterprises', 2017, <mneguidelines.oecd.org/RBC-for-Institutional-Investors.pdf>.

5 A Kelly, 'Brazil's "dirty list" names and shames companies involved in slave labour', *The Guardian*, 2013, <www.theguardian.com/sustainable-business/brazil-dirty-list-names-shames-slave-labour>.

6 International Labour Organization, National Pact for the Eradication of Slave Labour, 2018, <www.ilo.org/wcmsp5/groups/public/---dgreports/---ilo-washington/documents/genericdocument/wcms_189835.pdf>; A Feasley, 'Deploying disclosure laws to eliminate forced labour: Supply chain transparency efforts of Brazil and the United States of America', *Anti Trafficking Review*, no. 5, 2015, pp. 1–11, <www.antitraffickingreview.org/index.php/atrjournal/article/view/135>.

7 U Bacchi, 'Britain behind in anti-slavery fight due to lack of victim support-report', *Thomson Reuters Foundation News*, 2018, <news.trust.org/item/20181206164514-kdq0s/>.

8 N Uddin, 'The fight against modern slavery and human trafficking', *Winston Churchill Memorial Trust*, 2017, <www.wcmt.org.uk/fellows/reports/fight-against-modern-slavery-and-human-trafficking>.

9 K Guilbert, 'Hundreds of trafficked children go missing from UK care', *Thomson Reuters Foundation News*, 2018, <news.trust.org/item/20181219170931-4fzv8/>.

10 C Baker, J Hunter, Every Child Protected Against Trafficking UK & Missing People, 'Still in harm's way: An update report on trafficked and unaccompanied children going missing from care in the UK', Every Child Protected Against Trafficking UK, 2018, <www.ecpat.org.uk/still-in-harms-way>.

11 K Guilbert, 'Slaves to students: British college marks new start or survivors', *Thomson Reuters Foundation News*, 2018, <news.trust.org/item/20181128005717-rawaz/>.

12 J Cockayne, 'Secretariat Briefing Paper 3 Innovation for Inclusion: Using digital technology to increase financial agency and prevent modern slavery', Financial Sector Commission, 2019, <www.financialsectorcommission.org/wp-content/uploads/2019/03/BriefingPaper3.pdf>.

13 C Arup, C Beaton-Wells & J Paul-Taylor, 'Regulating supermarkets: The competition for space', *University of New South Wales Law Journal*, vol. 40, no. 3, 2017, pp. 1035–71.

14 D Segal, 'Syrian refugees toil on turkey's hazelnut farms with little to show for it', *New York Times*, 2019, <www.nytimes.com/2019/04/29/business/syrian-refugees-turkey-hazelnut-farms.html?smid=fb-nytimes&smtyp=cur>.
15 Segal 2019.
16 P Barrett & D Baumann-Pauly, 'Made in Ethiopia: Challenges in the garment industry's new frontier', NYU Stern Centre for Business and Human Rights, 2019, <www.stern.nyu.edu/experience-stern/faculty-research/made-ethiopia-challenges-garment-industry-s-new-frontier>.
17 B Pennell & R Segal, 'Tuzamurane Pineapple Cooperative, Rwanda', Oxfam, 2018, <oxfamilibrary.openrepository.com/bitstream/handle/10546/620422/cs-tuzamurane-pineapple-cooperative-rwanda-210618-en.pdf?sequence=1>.
18 European Commission, 'European semester thematic factsheet', 2017, <ec.europa.eu/info/sites/info/files/file_import/european-semester_thematic-factsheet_public-procurement_en_0.pdf>.
19 E Conlon, 'Modern slavery: Do the 2014 EU Procurement Directives establish new routes to remedy for victims?', International Learning Lab on Public Procurement and Human Rights, 2018, <www.hrprocurementlab.org/blog/modern-slavery-do-the-2014-eu-procurement-directives-establish-new-routes-to-remedy-for-victims/>.
20 O Martin-Ortega & C M O'Brien, 'The SDGs, human rights and procurement: An urgent need for policy coherence' in UNOPS, *High Impact Procurement, United National Office for Project Services*, 2017, <content.unops.org/publications/ASR/ASR-supplement-2016_EN.pdf?mtime=20171214185155>.
21 The Global Slavery Index, 'Country Data, Greece', 2018, <www.globalslaveryindex.org/2018/data/country-data/greece/>.
22 K Guilbert, 'Athens aims to deliver gods and services free of forced labour', *Thomson Reuters Foundation News*, 2019, <news.trust.org/item/20190130173827-ot6xj/>.
23 'Italy's far-right government turns away rescue ship with 224 refugees: "They will only see Italy on a postcard"', *Independent*, 2018, <www.independent.co.uk/news/world/europe/migrant-crisis-italy-rescue-ships-matteo-salvini-libya-spain-latest-mission-lifeline-a8412591.html>.
24 Undercurrent News, 'Activist Andy Hall ordered to pay $310k to Thai pineapple company', May 2019, < https://www.undercurrentnews.com/2019/05/22/activist-andy-hall-ordered-to-

pay-310k-to-thai-pineapple-company/>.

25 S Phasuk, 'Thai court acquits migrant workers of defamation', *Human Rights Watch*, 2018, <www.hrw.org/news/2018/07/12/thai-court-acquits-migrant-workers-defamation>.

26 A Kelly, 'Thai seafood: Are the prawns on your plate still fished by slaves?, *The Guardian*, 2018, <www.theguardian.com/global-development/2018/jan/23/thai-seafood-industry-report-trafficking-rights-abuses>.

27 Outland Denim, 'Our story', 2019, <www.outlanddenim.com.au/page/our-story/; tonyschocolonely.com/nl/nl>.

28 J Catsoulis, '"Invisible Hands" review: The children fueling global capitalism', *New York Times*, 2018, <www.nytimes.com/2018/11/22/movies/invisible-hands-review.html>.

29 S Elks, 'Major brands practise "wilful ignorance" over child slaves – filmmaker', *Thomson Reuters*, 2018, <af.reutersmedia.net/article/ghanaNews/idAFL8N1XW3W0>.

30 Focus on Labour Exploitation, 'Full disclosure: New report explores modern slavery reporting', 2019, <www.labourexploitation.org/news/full-disclosure-new-report-explores-modern-slavery-reporting>.

31 Business & Human Rights Resource Centre, 'Press release: FTSE 100 failing to lead on eliminating modern slavery from supply chains?', 2017, <www.business-humanrights.org/en/press-release-ftse-100-failing-to-lead-on-eliminating-modern-slavery-from-supply-chains>.

32 Kelly 2018.

33 Human Rights Watch, 'Hidden chains: Rights abuses and forced labor in Thailand's fishing industry', 2018, <www.hrw.org/report/2018/01/23/hidden-chains/rights-abuses-and-forced-labor-thailands-fishing-industry>.

34 A Boleyn, 'A matter of trust in Good Business' in Qantas, *Qantas Spirit of Australia Travel Magazine*, April 2019.

35 L Fink, 'Chairman's Lettler', BlackRock, 2018, <www.blackrock.com/corporate/investor-relations/larry-fink-chairmans-letter>.

36 D Kinley, *Necessary Evil: How to Fix Finance by Saving Human Rights*, Oxford University Press, Oxford, 2018.

37 J Cajal-Grossi, R Macchiavello & G Noguera, 'International buyers' sourcing and suppliers' markups in Bangladeshi garments', Discussion Paper No 1598, Centre for Economic Performance, January 2019.

38 M Castells, *The Power of Identity: The Information Age: Economy,*

Society, and Culture, John Wiley & Sons, 2nd edn, vol. 2, 2010, p. 417.

39 D Arenas, J M Lozano & L Albareda, 'The role of NGOs in CSR: Mutual perceptions among stakeholders', Journal of Business Ethics, vol. 88, no. 1, 2009, pp. 175–97.

40 E Arengo, *Future of Fashion: Worker led strategies for corporate accountability in the global apparel industry*, International Labor Rights Forum, 2019, p. 28.

41 Milk with Dignity Standards Council, 'About', Milk with Dignity, 2019, <milkwithdignity.org/about>.

42 International Trade Union Confederation, '2018 ITUC Global Rights Index', 2018, <www.ituc-csi.org/IMG/pdf/ituc-global-rights-index-2018-en-final-2.pdf>.

43 D Vaughan-Whitehead & LP Caro, 'Purchasing practices and working conditions in global supply chains: Global survey results', International Labour Organization, 2017, <www.ilo.org/wcmsp5/groups/public/---ed_protect/---protrav/---travail/documents/publication/wcms_556336.pdf>.

44 K Guilbert, 'World needs workers' rights "revolution" to end modern slavery – experts', *Thomson Reuters Foundation News*, 2018, <news.trust.org/item/20181103192323-xyfyj/>.

45 C Louche & T Hebb, 'SRI in the 21st century: Does it make a difference to society?', *Critical Studies on Corporate Responsibility, Governance and Sustainability*, vol. 7, 2014, pp. 275–97.

46 DE Schwartz, 'The public-interest proxy contest: Reflections on Campaign GM', *Michigan Law Review*, vol. 69, no. 3, 1971, pp. 419–538; R Sparkes, *Socially Responsible Investment: A Global Revolution*, John Wiley and Sons, Chichester, 2002, p. 50.

47 MJ Bekink, 'Thinking long-term: Investment strategies and responsibility' cited in D Baumann-Pauly & J Nolan (eds), *Business and Human Rights: From Principles to Practice*, Routledge, 2016, p. 228; California Public Employees Retirement System, 'Investment and pension funding: Facts at a glance for fiscal year 2016–2017', 2017. CalPERS specifies its 'Total fund market value' as at the end of the 2016/17 financial year as being US$326.4 billion.

48 At the end of 2016, the Norwegian Fund's market value was NOK7507 billion. Norwegian Ministry of Finance, 'Meld. St. 26 (2016–2017): The Management of the Government Pension Fund in 2016', 31 March 2017, p. 9.

49 G Vasudeva, 'Weaving together the normative and regulative roles

of government: How the Norwegian Sovereign Wealth Fund's responsible conduct is shaping firms' cross-border investments', *Organization Science*, vol. 24, no. 6, 2013, pp. 1662–82, 1664; D Reiche, 'Sovereign wealth funds as a new instrument of climate protection policy? A case study of Norway as a pioneer of ethical guidelines for investment policy', *Energy*, vol. 35, no. 9, 2010, pp. 3569–77, p. 3570.

50 C O'Connor & S Labowitz, Putting the 'S' in ESG: Measuring human rights performance for investors, NYU Stern Centre for Business and Human Rights, New York, 2017, Foreword.

51 Shareaction, 'Forced labour: What investors need to know', 2016, <shareaction.org/wp-content/uploads/2016/06/ForcedLabour-InvestorBriefing.pdf>.

52 J Sloggett & B Reinboth, 'ESG integration: How are social issues influencing investment decisions', Your Socially Responsible Investment, 2017, <yoursri.com/media-new/download/pri_a-practical-guide-to-esg-integration_social_2017.pdf>.

53 Know the Chain, '2018 information and communications technology benchmark findings report', 2018, <knowthechain.org/wp-content/uploads/KTC-ICT-May2018-Final.pdf>.

54 S George, 'Is CSR dead? How millennials are driving demand for authentic brand purpose', *Edie.net*, 2018, <www.edie.net/library/Is-CSR-dead--How-millennials-are-creating-demand-for-brand-purpose/6848>.

55 T Devinney, P Auger & G Eckhardt, *The Myth of the Ethical Consumer*, Cambridge University Press, Cambridge, 2010.

56 Baptist World Aid Australia, 'Ethical fashion guide', 2019, <baptistworldaid.org.au/resources/2019-ethical-fashion-guide/>.

57 K Guilbert, 'Cooperation, not cash, key to ending modern slavery by 2030 – experts', *Thomson Reuters Foundation News*, 2018, <news.trust.org/item/20181002194340-82oxr/>.

58 TISCREPORT, 'UK city transparency report', <tiscreport.org/public-sector/uk-transparency-report/>.

59 K Guilbert, 'World backs data "revolution" in global anti-slavery drive', *Thomson Reuters Foundation News*, 2018, <news.trust.org/item/20181024160615-cbz3d/>.

60 E Wulfhorst, 'Data project aims to stop human trafficking before it occurs – organisers', *Thomson Reuters Foundation News*, 2018, <news.trust.org/item/20181018185940-85jmj/>.

61 K Guilbert, 'London calling: Facebook and banks enlisted in drive to stop slavery', *Thomson Reuters Foundation News*, 2018, <news.

trust.org/item/20181203045654-3ppfp/>.
62 A Ahuja, 'Surveillance from the skies may help fight against modern slavery', *Financial Times*, 2019, <www.ft.com/content/e16ea530-39b5-11e9-9988-28303f70fcff?desktop=true&segmentId=7c8f09b9-9b61-4fbb-9430-9208a9e233c>.
63 Rights Lab, 'Slavery from space', *Zooniverse*, <www.zooniverse.org/projects/ezzjcw/rights-lab-slavery-from-space>.
64 GM Foody, F Ling, DS Boyd, X Li & J Wardlaw, 'Earth observation and machine learning to meet Sustainable Development Goal 8.7 mapping sites associated with slavery from space', *Remote Sensing*, vol. 11, no. 3, 2019, pp. 266–78, <www.mdpi.com/2072-4292/11/3/266/htm>.
65 B Farbenblum, L Berg & A Kintominas, 'Transformative technology for migrant workers: Opportunities, challenges and risks', Open Society Foundations, November 2018.
66 Farbenblum, Berg & Kintominas, 2018, p. 21.

Index

Index

MIX
Papier | Fördert gute Waldnutzung
FSC® C083411

Zeitfracht Medien GmbH
Ferdinand-Jühlke-Straße 7
99095 Erfurt, Deutschland
produktsicherheit@kolibri360.de